Math Bafflers

Logic Puzzles That Use Real-World Math

Grades 6–8

Math Bafflers

Logic Puzzles That Use Real-World Math

Marilynn L. Rapp Buxton

Routledge
Taylor & Francis Group

NEW YORK AND LONDON

First published in 2011 by Prufrock Press Inc.

Published in 2021 by Routledge
605 Third Avenue, New York, NY 10017
2 Park Square, Milton Park, Abingdon, Oxon OX14 4RN

Routledge is an imprint of the Taylor & Francis Group, an informa business

Copyright © 2011 Taylor & Francis Group

Layout design by Raquel Trevino

Illustrations by Joshua Krezinski

ISBN: 9781032141633 (hbk)
ISBN: 9781593637125 (hbk)

DOI: 10.4324/9781003236382

Table of Contents

Puzzles

> Puzzles at the beginning of this list are easier to solve than the ones that come later in the list—but besides that, they are in no particular order. Puzzles at the end require you to use the logical thinking processes that you learned while solving the easier puzzles. Good luck!

Note to Teachers

Many college professors and business professionals have told me, "Teach kids how to think and ask them to work hard." I teach elementary gifted and talented students in addition to teaching thinking skills in classrooms. Students in these classes learn creative thinking (e.g., fluency, flexibility, originality, elaboration, problem solving) and critical thinking (e.g., labeling, observation, analogies, classification, webbing, comparison, circle logic, syllogisms, cause and effect, patterning, sequencing, table logic, matrix logic). Students enjoy logic puzzles so much that they request more of them!

But how can a teacher justify using logic puzzles when standards must be met? Do you have students who finish assignments quickly (especially math assignments) and then ask, "What should I do now?" What if you had a logic book that reinforced math concepts?

This book is unique in that it requires students to use logical reasoning and perform a variety of operations and skills that align with state and national math standards (including standards for fractions, decimals, estimating, exponents, sequencing, algebra, time, percentages, measurement, area, and money). Students will read for details, make hypotheses, draw conclusions, organize information, and use syllogistic thinking. Teachers can feel confident that they are providing high-level thinking and rigor while reinforcing required skills in a format that students enjoy.

As I was creating this book, I enlisted the help of real students, who field tested puzzles and suggested topics that other kids would enjoy. As noted in the Table of Contents, the earlier puzzles in the book are easier, whereas the later puzzles are more challenging.

Students should be able to work independently on these problems. They should read the explanation of the logic process, apply the strategies described on p. 4, try the sample problem, begin with simpler puzzles, heed the instructions in introductory paragraphs, and note any hints for solving.

The solutions provided contain step-by-step explanations of my own reasoning; however, other solvers may use different paths of reasoning that also yield correct solutions. Teachers and parents may use the included solutions as an answer key, or they may allow students to self-check and clarify their reasoning.

This book may be used as alternative work during compacting, as enrichment, in centers, or just for fun. Students may work alone, with partners, in small groups, or in whatever arrangement best suits the needs of teachers and students. A student who fully understands the reasoning of a particular puzzle could demonstrate it to the rest of the class.

I hope that this book will be a helpful resource for teachers who strive to provide challenging, applicable, and practical math enrichment that is enjoyable for students who love to think!

How to Solve the Math Bafflers

Logic is a kind of critical thinking, an essential life skill. Using logic within a given content area is an effective way to integrate critical thinking, problem solving, and higher level processes into your everyday thought. Solving the puzzles in *Math Bafflers* promotes logic, reading for detail, analysis, making assumptions, and drawing valid conclusions in complex, real-life situations. Individuals who have strong critical thinking skills can make sense out of multiple pieces of information.

Read the following typical family scenario:

> Betty's Tuesday saxophone lesson is 60 minutes earlier than Nadine's Thursday tennis lesson, but Betty's Thursday swimming lesson is 30 minutes later than Nadine's Wednesday trumpet lesson. Also, Everett's Monday tuba lesson is earlier than Nadine's Thursday tennis lesson, and Everett's Friday racquetball lesson is 60 minutes earlier than Nadine's Wednesday music lesson.

Whew! That seems overwhelming. However, by organizing that scenario into individual clues and placing the information in a visual format, students can easily make sense of that confusing schedule. The logic used to solve the puzzles in *Math Bafflers* is similar to matrix logic, but the graphic is different.

Steps for Solving a Math Baffler

1. Read the introductory paragraph. It outlines the situation and contains necessary information.
2. Read each clue and use the information to make corresponding changes to the chart.
3. Each column represents a specific person or part of the situation in the problem. When a clue mentions a certain person or thing shown in a column, circle the appropriate item(s) listed in that column. For example, if a clue says that Ben is 11 years old, then under "Ben," you should circle "11 years." Items in the same section that are above, below, or next to the circled item must be crossed out, because they are no longer possibilities (e.g., Ben cannot also be 10 years old or 12 years old). It is very important that you always remember to do this!

4. Also use the clues to cross out items in a column that do not belong or are not possibilities. For example, if a clue tells you that Alicia is not 12 years old, then under "Alicia," cross out "12 years."

5. When there is only one item remaining in a certain column or row, then circle it. There will not be any more clues about it.

6. Once you have only one item circled in each row of each section, and only one in each column within a section, then you have solved the puzzle.

7. Check the solutions listed in the back of the book to make sure that you solved the puzzle correctly. If you have trouble solving a puzzle, or if you get incorrect answers, then read the description in the back of the book about how the puzzle could be solved. (It is possible, however, to solve the puzzle using slightly different reasoning.) At the end of each description in the Solutions section is a summary listing only the correct answers.

Strategies to Help You Solve the Math Bafflers

1. Always read introductory paragraphs. This paragraph describes the situation, and it may contain essential information that is not available in a clue. For example, the introductory paragraph might say, "Three students (a girl named Avery, a girl named Chris, and a boy named Pat) live in Napa." Then, a clue might tell you that a girl lives on Ash Street. After reading the introductory paragraph, you know that because Pat is a boy, he cannot live on Ash Street.

2. Be alert for clues about gender. Avery, Chris, and Pat are not gender-specific names. Recall introductory information when marking for a clue, such as "The girls do not like grapes." From the introduction, you know that Pat is a boy, so he likes grapes. Notice details such as gender pronouns in clues. For example, "*His* wallet contained $6.45." This means that a boy has $6.45, so no girl has $6.45.

3. Read, organize, and consider information from every clue. Each clue is essential for solving the puzzle. "Henry does not own a dog" may seem pointless. However, a later clue may tell you, "The one who owns the dog made $8 babysitting." Because Henry does not own a dog, he is not the one who made $8 babysitting.

4. There is sufficient information in the clues to solve every puzzle, but sometimes the logic is complex. Do not guess or assume. All of your conclusions should be backed up by proof from the clues and introductions.

5.   Some of the Math Bafflers require you to perform mathematical calculations or fill in numbers. If you like, you should check the Solutions section in the back of the book to make sure you have the correct numbers before you go on to solve the puzzle.

6.   Some puzzles can be solved from reading through all of the clues and doing the corresponding math operations just once. However, some of the Math Bafflers require you to go back and read through the clues again so that you can apply information from the later clues to the earlier clues. If necessary, reread clues and use further reasoning.

7.   Use *syllogistic thinking* when you are marking items. *Syllogisms* have two premises and a conclusion. For example, one clue might say, "Susan drank half a cup of water." Another clue might say, "The one who drank half a cup of water ate ¼ of an apple." From these two premises, you can conclude that Susan ate ¼ of an apple.

8.   Use *sequential thinking* to mark items with clues involving the order in which something happened. For instance, "Mary arrived after Jennifer, but before Connie." Write the different parts of the clue down in order: Jennifer, then Mary, and then Connie. A clue like "Roy is 2 years older than Fred, who is 3 years older than Susan" gives specific age differences. Write them in order. Then, once you know one age, you can get the others.

9.   Notice items mentioned in multiple clues. Connect these pieces of information to draw conclusions.

10.   A clue like "Neither Rob nor the nurse is 5 ft 9 in. tall" gives you information about three different people: Rob isn't the nurse, the nurse isn't 5 ft 9 in., and Rob isn't 5 ft 9 in.

11.   In a clue like "There are four people: one who spent $3, the girl with blue eyes, the one who bought a soda, and Tania," you know that you are talking about four different people and that none of these pieces of information overlap with others. The person who spent $3 is different than the girl with blue eyes, who is different than the one who bought a soda, who is not Tania (and Tania did not spend $3, does not have blue eyes, and so forth).

Practice Problem

Try the following sample puzzle. For each clue, cross out items that do not belong or are not possibilities. In the provided solutions, when something is in brackets, it means that whatever the brackets enclose was learned in an earlier clue. For example, [3] means that something relevant was learned in Clue

3. If something is in parentheses—or is followed by "(only one)"—it means that this is the only choice remaining in a column or row, and you should circle it. For example, "Miss Fay matches up with Wednesday (only one)" means that Wednesday is the only item not crossed out in either the row or column for Miss Fay, and you should circle it.

Three siblings are all both musically and physically talented. Each sibling has a private music lesson and a private sports lesson on a different day and time each week. Read the clues to discover the time that each sibling has his or her music lesson and sports lesson.

	Betty	Everett	Nadine
Music	3:30 p.m.	3:30 p.m.	3:30 p.m.
	4:00 p.m.	4:00 p.m.	4:00 p.m.
	~~5:30 p.m.~~	5:30 p.m.	5:30 p.m.
Sports	4:30 p.m.	4:30 p.m.	4:30 p.m.
	5:00 p.m.	5:00 p.m.	5:00 p.m.
	6:00 p.m.	6:00 p.m.	~~6:00 p.m.~~

Clue 1: Betty's Tuesday saxophone lesson is 60 min earlier than Nadine's Thursday tennis lesson.

Reasoning: If Betty's music lesson were at 5:30, then Nadine's sport would be at 6:30, and that is not a choice. Cross out 5:30 for Betty's music time. Cross out 6:00 for Nadine's sport time (no 5:00 music for Betty).

	Betty	Everett	Nadine
Music	3:30 p.m.	3:30 p.m.	~~3:30 p.m.~~
	4:00 p.m.	4:00 p.m.	4:00 p.m.
	~~5:30 p.m.~~	5:30 p.m.	5:30 p.m.
Sports	4:30 p.m.	4:30 p.m.	4:30 p.m.
	~~5:00 p.m.~~	5:00 p.m.	5:00 p.m.
	6:00 p.m.	6:00 p.m.	~~6:00 p.m.~~

Clue 2: Betty's Thursday swimming lesson is 30 min later than Nadine's Wednesday trumpet lesson.

Reasoning: If Nadine's music lesson were at 3:30, then Betty's sport would be at 4:00, and that is not a choice. Cross out 3:30 for Nadine's music time. Cross out 5:00 for Betty's sport time (no 4:30 music time for Nadine).

	Betty	Everett	Nadine
Music	3:30 p.m. 4:00 p.m. ~~5:30 p.m.~~	3:30 p.m. 4:00 p.m. ~~5:30 p.m.~~	~~3:30 p.m.~~ ~~4:00 p.m.~~ (5:30 p.m.)
Sports	~~4:30 p.m.~~ ~~5:00 p.m.~~ (6:00 p.m.)	4:30 p.m. 5:00 p.m. ~~6:00 p.m.~~	4:30 p.m. 5:00 p.m. ~~6:00 p.m.~~

Clue 3: Everett's Monday tuba lesson is earlier than Nadine's Thursday tennis lesson.

Reasoning: Nadine has a 4:30 or 5:00 sport [2], so Everett's music lesson is earlier than 5:00. Cross out his 5:30 music time. (Nadine's music lesson is at 5:30 because it is the only one remaining in that row, so circle it). Cross out the 4:00 music time for Nadine. Betty's sport is at 6:00, because it is 30 min later than Nadine's music lesson [2]. Circle it. Cross out Betty's 4:30 sport time. Cross out Everett's 6:00 sport time.

	Betty	Everett	Nadine
Music	~~3:30 p.m.~~ (4:00 p.m.) ~~5:30 p.m.~~	(3:30 p.m.) ~~4:00 p.m.~~ ~~5:30 p.m.~~	~~3:30 p.m.~~ ~~4:00 p.m.~~ (5:30 p.m.)
Sports	~~4:30 p.m.~~ ~~5:00 p.m.~~ (6:00 p.m.)	(4:30 p.m.) ~~5:00 p.m.~~ ~~6:00 p.m.~~	~~4:30 p.m.~~ (5:00 p.m.) ~~6:00 p.m.~~

Clue 4: Everett's Friday racquetball lesson is 60 min earlier than Nadine's Wednesday music lesson.

Reasoning: Nadine's music lesson is at 5:30 [3], so Everett's sport is at 4:30. Circle it. Cross out his 5:00 sport time and Nadine's 4:30 sport time. Nadine has a 5:00 sport (only one)—circle it. Betty's music lesson is at 4:00, because it is 60 min earlier than Nadine's 5:00 sport [1]. Cross out Betty's 3:30 music time. (Everett has a 3:30 music lesson.) Cross out Everett's 4:00 music time.

Solution: Betty, 4:00 music lesson, 6:00 sport; Everett, 3:30 music lesson, 4:30 sport; Nadine, 5:30 music lesson, 5:00 sport.

Congratulations for practicing your reasoning skills, and have fun solving these Math Bafflers!

Who Will Be My Teacher?

Several teachers at Clark Beach Middle School have taught at their current grade levels for a number of years. To give themselves some variety and challenge, they all decided to make a switch and teach an elementary grade level next year. (At Clark Beach, grades 1–4 are elementary school, and grades 5–8 are middle school.) Use the clues to find out each teacher's current grade level and what grade he or she will teach next year.

Clues:

1. Mrs. Thomsen does not teach fifth grade now and will not teach fourth grade next fall.
2. Ms. Nixon teaches either fifth or seventh grade now, but she will not teach second grade next year.
3. Neither Mr. Clausing nor the one who will teach second grade next year is currently the sixth-grade teacher.
4. Ms. Nixon does not teach seventh grade and will not teach third or fourth grade next fall.
5. Neither Mrs. Thomsen nor the one who will teach second grade next year is teaching seventh grade now.

	Mr. Clausing	Mrs. Harris	Ms. Nixon	Mrs. Thomsen
Current Grade	fifth grade sixth grade seventh grade eighth grade	fifth grade sixth grade seventh grade eighth grade	fifth grade sixth grade seventh grade eighth grade	fifth grade sixth grade seventh grade eighth grade
Next Year's Grade	first grade second grade third grade fourth grade	first grade second grade third grade fourth grade	first grade second grade third grade fourth grade	first grade second grade third grade fourth grade

Face-Bond Friends

Braxton, Kaela, Trexi, and Viola are close friends, but they have never met. They are Internet Face-Bond friends who all have one friend in common, plus many other Face-Bond friends. They live in four different towns, but one day they decided to drive to a town about midway between all of their towns and meet for the first time. Each girl drove a different number of miles. Read the clues to figure out how far each girl drove and how many Face-Bond friends she has.

Clues:

1. The one with 37 Face-Bond friends drove half as far as Braxton.
2. Viola drove farther than Kaela, but half as far as the girl with 34 Face-Bond friends.
3. The one with 29 Face-Bond friends drove 150 miles.
4. Trexi drove 50 miles less than the one with 34 Face-Bond friends, but twice as far as the one with 46 Face-Bond friends.

		Braxton	Kaela	Trexi	Viola
Number of Friends		29	29	29	29
		34	34	34	34
		37	37	37	37
		46	46	46	46
Distance Traveled		75 mi	75 mi	75 mi	75 mi
		100 mi	100 mi	100 mi	100 mi
		150 mi	150 mi	150 mi	150 mi
		200 mi	200 mi	200 mi	200 mi

DOI: 10.4324/9781003236382-3

Brr! Baby, It's Cold Outside

It is winter! That means snow and negative temperatures in the northern states. Cousins from three different cities monitored Fahrenheit temperatures for 6 days straight during a cold snap. Nobody recorded the same temperature on any of the 6 days. Read the clues and record which temperatures each cousin reported for each day.

Clues:

1. Odell recorded a 7-degree drop in temperature from Sunday to Monday.
2. Wendy recorded a 7-degree decrease in temperature from Tuesday to Wednesday.
3. It warmed up 9 degrees from Thursday to Friday in Fargo, ND, according to Odell.
4. Harriett noticed a unique pattern in her weather report. It warmed up 1 degree between Sunday and Monday, it warmed up 1 degree between Tuesday and Wednesday, and it warmed up 1 degree between Thursday and Friday.

	Harriet	Odell	Wendy
Sunday	−1 −6 −10	−1 −6 −10	−1 −6 −10
Monday	−5 −8 −12	−5 −8 −12	−5 −8 −12
Tuesday	−4 −15 −18	−4 −15 −18	−4 −15 −18
Wednesday	−11 −14 −20	−11 −14 −20	−11 −14 −20
Thursday	−3 −13 −16	−3 −13 −16	−3 −13 −16
Friday	−2 −7 −9	−2 −7 −9	−2 −7 −9

Please Don't Take My Sunshine Away

"Eight-O is Great-O!" is the motto of Florida's Sunshine Club. Members promote good health by walking, especially when it is a comfortable 80 degrees outside. But one new resident who moved from Alaska thought 80 degrees was too warm. "I am going to think in terms of Celsius, a different temperature scale," she said. "That will make me feel cooler," she claimed.

Look at the high temperatures that were recorded for each day last week. Convert Fahrenheit to Celsius and Celsius to Fahrenheit by using the formulas in the box at the left of the chart. Round Fahrenheit temperatures to the nearest whole numbers and Celsius temperatures to the nearest hundredths. Write down your conversions in the spaces provided.

Examples:
$100°$ C is _____ $°$ F.
$(\frac{9}{5} \times 100) + 32$
$\frac{9}{5}$ is 1.8, so 1.8 x 100, which is 180, + 32 = $212°$
$100°$ F is _____ $°$ C.
$\frac{5}{9} \times (100 - 32)$
$\frac{5}{9}$ is $.\overline{5}$ (.555 . . .), so $.\overline{5}$ x 68 = $37.78°$

Then read the clues to determine each club member's favorite temperature that was recorded as the high during one day last week.

Clues:

1. Dharma's favorite day was warmer than Bina's, but cooler than Terrence's.
2. Adriel's best day was when the Fahrenheit temperature was $3°$ F higher than on Shinichi's favorite day.
3. Bina's best day was warmer than Ethan's perfect day, but cooler than Neva's perfect day.
4. Neva loved the day the Fahrenheit temperature was $4°$ less than it was on Terrence's favorite day.
5. Adriel celebrated the day the Celsius temperature was $1.67°$ less than it was on Neva's best day.
6. Shinichi loved the day the Celsius temperature was $1.11°$ warmer than it was on Bina's ideal day.

Please Don't Take My Sunshine Away, continued

Celsius ▶	25.56°	°	28.33°	°	30°	°	33.89°
Fahrenheit ▶	°	81°	°	85°	°	89°	°
Fahrenheit = $(\%_5 \times C°) + 32$ **Celsius =** $\%_9 \times$ (F° – 32)	Adriel Bina Dharma Ethan Neva Shinichi Terrence	Adriel Bina Dharma Ethan Neva Shinichi Terrence	Adriel Bina Dharma Ethan Neva Shinichi Terrence	Adriel Bina Dharma Ethan Neva Shinichi Terrence	Adriel Bina Dharma Ethan Neva Shinichi Terrence	Adriel Bina Dharma Ethan Neva Shinichi Terrence	Adriel Bina Dharma Ethan Neva Shinichi Terrence

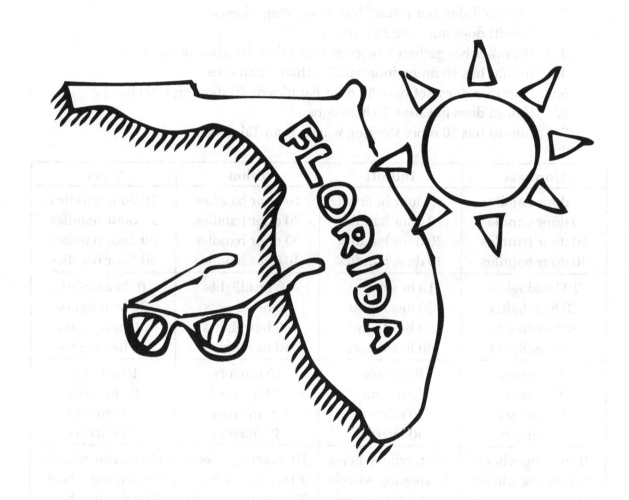

Century Club

The Century Club is made up of people who collect 100 of any type of item. Four people have each collected 100 various useable car parts over the years, and so they are eligible for the club. Each of these four collectors was given a car name as a baby and has been interested in cars for his or her entire life. Each is displaying a combination of door handles, headlights, mirrors, and steering wheels. Nobody has the same number of any item, and each person has exactly 100 items. Use the clues to discover how many of each car part each member has. (Hint: This means that to complete the puzzle, once you circle 20 for any person, you can eliminate 20 for the other car part options, and so on.)

Clues:

1. Neither Talon nor Infiniti has 30 steering wheels.
2. Infiniti does not have 20 mirrors.
3. Hummer has gathered twice as many door handles as Viper has.
4. Infiniti has 10 more door handles than Talon does.
5. Hummer does not have 40 door handles or 40 steering wheels.
6. Infiniti does not have 30 headlights.
7. Infiniti has 10 more steering wheels than Talon has.

Hummer	Infiniti	Talon	Viper
10 door handles	10 door handles	10 door handles	10 door handles
20 door handles	20 door handles	20 door handles	20 door handles
30 door handles	30 door handles	30 door handles	30 door handles
40 door handles	40 door handles	40 door handles	40 door handles
10 headlights	10 headlights	10 headlights	10 headlights
20 headlights	20 headlights	20 headlights	20 headlights
30 headlights	30 headlights	30 headlights	30 headlights
40 headlights	40 headlights	40 headlights	40 headlights
10 mirrors	10 mirrors	10 mirrors	10 mirrors
20 mirrors	20 mirrors	20 mirrors	20 mirrors
30 mirrors	30 mirrors	30 mirrors	30 mirrors
40 mirrors	40 mirrors	40 mirrors	40 mirrors
10 steering wheels	10 steering wheels	10 steering wheels	10 steering wheels
20 steering wheels	20 steering wheels	20 steering wheels	20 steering wheels
30 steering wheels	30 steering wheels	30 steering wheels	30 steering wheels
40 steering wheels	40 steering wheels	40 steering wheels	40 steering wheels

I'm Done! What Should I Do Now?

Ten students at Goodminds Academy are extremely quick learners. Their teacher provides challenging enrichment materials for them to do with partners when they are finished with their regular work. Last week, different students played a card game, a strategy game, a dice game, a board game, and a math puzzler. Read the clues to find out which students worked as partners last week and how many points each pair earned in its activity. (Hint: It will be helpful to write some notes about what you learn in the clues.)

Clues:

1. The strategy game players earned 156 points.
2. Eadin and Cass enjoyed playing a card game together.
3. Claudette did not make 204 points on her math puzzler.
4. Hayley and Noah were not partners. Neither played a strategy game.
5. Claudette, Karen, and Margaret are friends, but none of them worked together.
6. Margaret got three times as many points as the card players. Noah was not her partner.
7. Noah got twice as many points as Cass. He did a math puzzler.
8. Ronald scored six times as many points as Dave and Sharon.

Claudette	Eadin	Hayley	Margaret	Sharon
Cass	Cass	Cass	Cass	Cass
Dave	Dave	Dave	Dave	Dave
Karen	Karen	Karen	Karen	Karen
Noah	Noah	Noah	Noah	Noah
Ronald	Ronald	Ronald	Ronald	Ronald
26 points	26 points	26 points	26 points	26 points
52 points	52 points	52 points	52 points	52 points
104 points	104 points	104 points	104 points	104 points
156 points	156 points	156 points	156 points	156 points
204 points	204 points	204 points	204 points	204 points

24 Game®

Four friends played 24 Game® during a rainy day. Using the four numbers on a card, and using each of those four numbers only once, players arrange the numbers in any order and use any operations they can to make 24. The results of succeeding equations are not counted as additional numbers. There might be multiple solutions, and it may be necessary to use brackets and/or parentheses.

Example:
A card showing the numbers 2 – 2 – 4 – 6 could be solved as:
$(2 \div 2) \times (4 \times 6) = 24$
$1 \times 24 = 24$
or as:
$(6 \times 2) \times (4 - 2) = 24$
$12 \times 2 = 24$

First, finish the equations using the eight groups of digits below. Then use the clues to determine which set of numbers each student had during Game 1 and Game 2 of 24 Game˙.

1 – 5 – 7 – 8	4 – 5 – 7 – 8	1 – 6 – 8 – 9	1 – 6 – 8 – 8
$(7 + \underline{\hspace{0.5cm}}) \times$ (\underline{\hspace{0.5cm}} – \underline{\hspace{0.5cm}}) = 24	$(8 + \underline{\hspace{0.5cm}}) \times$ (7 – \underline{\hspace{0.5cm}}) = 24 $5 + 8 + \underline{\hspace{0.5cm}} + \underline{\hspace{0.5cm}}$ = 24	$1 + 9 + \underline{\hspace{0.5cm}} + \underline{\hspace{0.5cm}}$ = 24 $(9 - \underline{\hspace{0.5cm}}) \times$ (\underline{\hspace{0.5cm}} $\div$ \underline{\hspace{0.5cm}}) = 24	$[(\underline{\hspace{0.5cm}} + 1) - \underline{\hspace{0.5cm}}]$ $\times 8 = 24$
1 – 2 – 2 – 7	1 – 2 – 6 – 7	1 – 1 – 2 – 9	1 – 2 – 5 – 6
$(\underline{\hspace{0.5cm}} + \underline{\hspace{0.5cm}}) \times$ (\underline{\hspace{0.5cm}} – 1) = 24	$(1 + \underline{\hspace{0.5cm}}) \times$ (\underline{\hspace{0.5cm}} $\div$ 2) = 24	$(9 - \underline{\hspace{0.5cm}}) \times$ (\underline{\hspace{0.5cm}} + \underline{\hspace{0.5cm}}) = 24	$(1 + \underline{\hspace{0.5cm}}) \times$ (\underline{\hspace{0.5cm}} – 2) = 24

Clues:

1. Jerry and Paul had three digits in common in Game 2.
2. Tamara and Collene had three digits in common in Game 1, but they did not have 1 – 5 – 7 – 8.
3. Collene tried to get 24 by adding her numbers in Game 2, but they only totaled 12.
4. Paul and another player used only addition to get 24 in Game 1.
5. Either Collene or Paul used (6 – 2) x (5 + 1) = 24 in Game 2.
6. Tamara's and Jerry's Game 1 equations led to 8 x 3 = 24.

		Collene	Jerry	Paul	Tamara
Game 1		1 – 5 – 7 – 8	1 – 5 – 7 – 8	1 – 5 – 7 – 8	1 – 5 – 7 – 8
		4 – 5 – 7 – 8	4 – 5 – 7 – 8	4 – 5 – 7 – 8	4 – 5 – 7 – 8
		1 – 6 – 8 – 9	1 – 6 – 8 – 9	1 – 6 – 8 – 9	1 – 6 – 8 – 9
		1 – 6 – 8 – 8	1 – 6 – 8 – 8	1 – 6 – 8 – 8	1 – 6 – 8 – 8
Game 2		1 – 2 – 2 – 7	1 – 2 – 2 – 7	1 – 2 – 2 – 7	1 – 2 – 2 – 7
		1 – 2 – 6 – 7	1 – 2 – 6 – 7	1 – 2 – 6 – 7	1 – 2 – 6 – 7
		1 – 1 – 2 – 9	1 – 1 – 2 – 9	1 – 1 – 2 – 9	1 – 1 – 2 – 9
		1 – 2 – 5 – 6	1 – 2 – 5 – 6	1 – 2 – 5 – 6	1 – 2 – 5 – 6

Cha-Ching

The Robinson brothers challenged each other to save their allowances and spare change for 3 weeks. They were curious as to which brother would tally the most money. Calculate the values of each number of coins and write them in the column. Use the clues to match each boy with the denominations and amounts he earned. The chart on page 19 will help you keep track of the information.

Which brother had the greatest total after 3 weeks? _____

Clues:

1. Quinton had more nickels than Nigel, but fewer than Lancaster.
2. Quinton had more quarters than Lancaster, but fewer than Nigel.
3. Lancaster had 10 fewer dimes than Nigel had nickels.
4. Treyton saved $0.25 more in nickels than in dimes and $6.00 more in quarters than in nickels.
5. Quinton's total savings was $1.00 more than Treyton's.

Values	Lancaster	Nigel	Quinton	Treyton
$ _____	45 nickels	45 nickels	45 nickels	45 nickels
$ _____	48 nickels	48 nickels	48 nickels	48 nickels
$ _____	60 nickels	60 nickels	60 nickels	60 nickels
$ _____	69 nickels	69 nickels	69 nickels	69 nickels
$ _____	20 dimes	20 dimes	20 dimes	20 dimes
$ _____	38 dimes	38 dimes	38 dimes	38 dimes
$ _____	40 dimes	40 dimes	40 dimes	40 dimes
$ _____	46 dimes	46 dimes	46 dimes	46 dimes
$ _____	23 quarters	23 quarters	23 quarters	23 quarters
$ _____	26 quarters	26 quarters	26 quarters	26 quarters
$ _____	28 quarters	28 quarters	28 quarters	28 quarters
$ _____	33 quarters	33 quarters	33 quarters	33 quarters

Cha-Ching, continued

	# of Nickels	Value of Nickels	# of Dimes	Value of Dimes	# of Quarters	Value of Quarters	Total
Lancaster							
Nigel							
Quinton							
Treyton							

Rah, Rah! Go, Team!

Five families are basketball fans, but each family roots for a different team. Each team wears a different colored uniform and scored a different number of points during its last game of the season. Use the clues to match each family with its favorite team's mascot, colors, and score. (Hint: It will help if you list items in correct sequential order when you can and write possible scores beside them.)

Clues:

1. The Meyer and Upton families' mascots are animals, and white is the color of one of their teams. One of their teams had the fewest points during its last game, and the other of the teams was the Bears.
2. The Beane and Lance families' teams wear green. One of their teams had the most points during its last game.
3. The Cyclones scored 2 points more than the Sailors, who scored 2 points more than the Bears during their last game this season.
4. The Lance's team scored 2 points more than the Paulson's team, but 2 points fewer than the Beane's team.
5. The Cyclones do not have any red or white in their uniforms.
6. The Meyer's favorite team does not wear a uniform with any red or blue in it.
7. The Panthers scored 76 points in their last game.
8. The Bears scored higher than the Upton's team, the one that wears the red and white uniform.

	Beane	Lance	Meyer	Paulson	Upton
Team	Bears Cyclones Jaguars Panthers Sailors	Bears Cyclones Jaguars Panthers Sailors	Bears Cyclones Jaguars Panthers Sailors	Bears Cyclones Jaguars Panthers Sailors	Bears Cyclones Jaguars Panthers Sailors
Team Color	blue / red / white blue / green / red green / white green / blue red / white	blue / red / white blue / green / red green / white green / blue red / white	blue / red / white blue / green / red green / white green / blue red / white	blue / red / white blue / green / red green / white green / blue red / white	blue / red / white blue / green / red green / white green / blue red / white
Last Score	68 points 70 points 72 points 74 points 76 points	68 points 70 points 72 points 74 points 76 points	68 points 70 points 72 points 74 points 76 points	68 points 70 points 72 points 74 points 76 points	68 points 70 points 72 points 74 points 76 points

NBA Salaries Are Not Dribble

Professional athletes earn extraordinary amounts of money playing sports. Here are top salaries from three seasons. Some players played for more than one season. Read the clues. When you find out a player's salary, circle his name and salary under the correct season. Cross out horizontally for his other two seasons and vertically just for that player (nobody has more than one income per season). There are four correct answers for each season (column), so do not cross out vertically when you circle something, as you normally would. Find four players and salaries for each season. The players are Kobe Bryant, Tim Duncan, Kevin Garnett, Rashard Lewis, Tracy McGrady, Jermaine O'Neal, and Shaquille O'Neal.

Clues:

1. Kevin Garnett earned $2,167,956 less during the 2010–2011 season than Shaquille O'Neal got in the 2008–2009 season.
2. Rashard Lewis earned about $2.6 million less during the 2010–2011 season than Tim Duncan made in 2009–2010.
3. Kevin Garnett made nearly $3.4 million more than Jermaine O'Neal during 2008–2009.
4. Kobe Bryant made nearly $4.2 million more in 2009–2010 than Tim Duncan earned during 2010–2011.
5. Tracy McGrady made $2,067,061 more in 2009–2010 than Kobe Bryant did during the 2008–2009 season.

Math Bafflers: Logic Puzzles That Use Real-World Math • Grades 6–8

NBA Salaries Are Not Dribble, continued

2008–2009 Season		2009–2010 Season		2010–2011 Season	
Garnett	$18,832,044	Garnett	$18,832,044	Garnett	$18,832,044
Duncan	$18,835,381	Duncan	$18,835,381	Duncan	$18,835,381
Lewis	$19,573,511	Lewis	$19,573,511	Lewis	$19,573,511
S. O'Neal	$21,000,000	S. O'Neal	$21,000,000	S. O'Neal	$21,000,000
Bryant	$21,262,500	Bryant	$21,262,500	Bryant	$21,262,500
J. O'Neal	$21,372,000	J. O'Neal	$21,372,000	J. O'Neal	$21,372,000
Duncan	$22,183,218	Duncan	$22,183,218	Duncan	$22,183,218
J. O'Neal	$22,995,000	J. O'Neal	$22,995,000	J. O'Neal	$22,995,000
Bryant	$23,034,375	Bryant	$23,034,375	Bryant	$23,034,375
McGrady	$23,329,561	McGrady	$23,329,561	McGrady	$23,329,561
Garnett	$24,751,000	Garnett	$24,751,000	Garnett	$24,751,000
Bryant	$24,806,250	Bryant	$24,806,250	Bryant	$24,806,250

Triple Trials

The Evans sisters—Brooke, age 11, Emma, age 10, and Natalie, age 9—were practicing metric measurements. They did three trials by guessing items in their home that might be a millimeter, a centimeter, and a meter long. Use the clues to find the lengths each girl guessed. To keep track of items, it may be helpful to write the item next to its size in the margin. Circle both the inches (in.) and metric measurements for each girl as you eliminate lengths.

Did you know . . .
1 millimeter (mm) is about as thick as a dime?
1 centimeter (1 cm; equal to 10 mm) is nearly the diameter of a dime?
1 meter (1 m; equal to 100 cm) is a little longer than a yardstick (39.37 in.)?

Convert inches to millimeters, centimeters, and meters, and write them in the boxes on page 25. Some are done for you.

Number of in. x 25.4 = mm
Number of in. x 2.54 = cm
Number of in. x .0254 = m

Clues:

1. One girl guessed that the ¼-in. button on her cell phone was about 1 mm.
2. The one who guessed that the 36-in. refrigerator was 1 m does not have a calculator.
3. Brooke guessed that the nib of her ink pen was 1 mm wide, but it was about 3.2 mm.
4. Natalie estimated that the ⅝-in. seam on her skirt was 1 cm.
5. One girl was helping her dad put up drywall. She thought the head of a ⅜-in. drywall screw was 1 cm and the 4-ft pieces of drywall might be 1 m wide.
6. The middle sister guessed that an M&M was 1 cm wide. It turned out to be about 1 ¼ cm.
7. Natalie's calculator has a thin 1/16-in. flip top. She thought it was 1 mm thick.

Triple Trials, continued

	Brooke		Emma		Natalie	
¹⁄₁₆ in.	.0625 in.	1.5875 mm	.0625 in.	1.5875 mm	.0625 in.	1.5875 mm
⅛ in.	.125 in.	_____mm	.125 in.	_____mm	.125 in.	_____mm
¼ in.	.25 in.	_____mm	.25 in.	_____mm	.25 in.	_____mm
⅜ in.	.375 in.	_____cm	.375 in.	_____cm	.375 in.	_____cm
½ in.	.5 in.	1.27 cm	.5 in.	1.27 cm	.5 in.	1.27 cm
⅝ in.	.625 in.	_____cm	.625 in.	_____cm	.625 in.	_____cm
1 yd	36 in.	_____ m	36 in.	_____ m	36 in.	_____ m
1 ¼ yd	45 in.	_____ m	45 in.	_____ m	45 in.	_____ m
1 ⅓ yd	48 in.	1.219 m	48 in.	1.219 m	48 in.	1.219 m

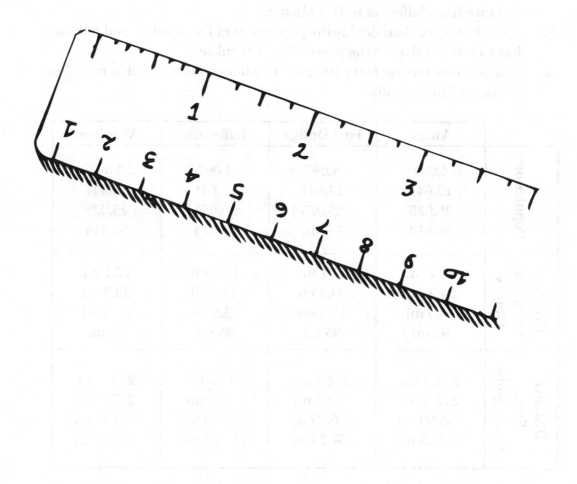

How Big and How Far?

Iowa Norman lives in Minneapolis, MN. She decided to research her name-sake state of Iowa, where her grandparents live. She compared four Iowa cities where she has relatives. First, she checked the population of each city. Next, she found the distance from each city to Des Moines, the capital of Iowa. Finally, she looked up the distance from each city to Minneapolis. See if you can match each city with its population, its distance from Des Moines, and its distance from Minneapolis.

Clues:

1. It is about 60 miles from Ames to Fort Dodge, but both cities are nearly the same distance from Minneapolis.
2. It is half as far from Waukee to Des Moines as it is from Ames to Des Moines.
3. Ames's population is a little less than 4 ½ times Waukee's population.
4. The distance from Jefferson to Minneapolis is 3 ½ times longer than the distance from Jefferson to Des Moines.
5. Ames has more than double the population of Fort Dodge, and Jefferson has a little less than ⅓ the population of Waukee.
6. It is 40 miles farther from Jefferson to Minneapolis than it is from Fort Dodge to Minneapolis.

	Ames	Fort Dodge	Jefferson	Waukee
Population	4,097 12,641 25,075 56,814	4,097 12,641 25,075 56,814	4,097 12,641 25,075 56,814	4,097 12,641 25,075 56,814
Distance From Des Moines	17.1 mi 34.3 mi 73.5 mi 95 mi	17.1 mi 34.3 mi 73.5 mi 95 mi	17.1 mi 34.3 mi 73.5 mi 95 mi	17.1 mi 34.3 mi 73.5 mi 95 mi
Distance From Minneapolis	214.3 mi 217.4 mi 256.99 mi 257.25 mi	214.3 mi 217.4 mi 256.99 mi 257.25 mi	214.3 mi 217.4 mi 256.99 mi 257.25 mi	214.3 mi 217.4 mi 256.99 mi 257.25 mi

Math Bafflers: Logic Puzzles That Use Real-World Math • Grades 6–8

Saturated Saturday

Four friends are very active youngsters. One Saturday, they were all involved in a swimming lesson at the local pool, a ball game with their league teams, and a picnic with their families. Nobody had any one activity during the same time that a friend had that activity, and each one stayed the full length of time at each event. Look at each amount of time and convert it to a fraction of hours. For example, 8:00–8:45 is ¾ of an hour. Use the clues to figure out each one's schedule for this very busy Saturday.

Clues:

1. The one who had a 1-hour swim lesson attended a 3 ½-hour picnic.
2. The one whose ball game started at 12:45 had a 45-minute swim lesson.
3. Floyd's swimming lesson started later than Horace's, but his ball game started earlier.
4. Jinjer's ball game took less time than Horace's ball game, but it started later.
5. The picnic Jinjer attended lasted longer than the picnic Horace attended.
6. Horace's swimming lesson was longer than Jinjer's, and Floyd's swim lesson was longer than Dixie's.

	Fractions	Dixie	Floyd	Horace	Jinjer
Swimming	¾ hr	8:00–8:45	8:00–8:45	8:00–8:45	8:00–8:45
	_____ hr	8:45–9:45	8:45–9:45	8:45–9:45	8:45–9:45
	_____ hr	9:30–10:00	9:30–10:00	9:30–10:00	9:30–10:00
	_____ hr	10:15–11:00	10:15–11:00	10:15–11:00	10:15–11:00
Ball Game	_____ hr	12:30–2:15	12:30–2:15	12:30–2:15	12:30–2:15
	_____ hr	12:45–2:00	12:45–2:00	12:45–2:00	12:45–2:00
	_____ hr	1:15–3:45	1:15–3:45	1:15–3:45	1:15–3:45
	_____ hr	1:30–3:45	1:30–3:45	1:30–3:45	1:30–3:45
Picnic	_____ hr	3:00–6:00	3:00–6:00	3:00–6:00	3:00–6:00
	_____ hr	3:30–7:00	3:30 7:00	3:30–7:00	3:30–7:00
	_____ hr	4:30–6:45	4:30–6:45	4:30–6:45	4:30–6:45
	_____ hr	5:00–6:45	5:00–6:45	5:00–6:45	5:00–6:45

Movies and Music Are Marvelous

Six people (three boys named Craig, Dale, and Franz, and three girls named Bethenny, Elizabeth, and Georgia) met music magnate Maxwell Marple. They mentioned to him that they all had a magnanimous magnetism to movies and music. They collect everything from Frank Sinatra and Doris Day records to material by current performers. Use the clues to find out the birth year of each music lover, as well as how many movies and music CDs he or she has collected.

Clues:

1. Craig is older than Dale and Elizabeth. Franz is younger than Georgia and Bethenny.
2. Georgia has three times as many CDs as movies, and none of the boys has twice as many CDs as he has movies.
3. Craig is 10 years older than Bethenny, and Dale is 10 years older than Franz.
4. Craig has three times as many CDs as he has movies. He has fewer CDs than Georgia, but more than Dale.
5. Dale has 20 fewer movies than Bethenny, and Franz has 20 fewer movies than Craig.
6. The youngest person does not have the fewest CDs.
7. The one born in 1982 does not have 82 CDs, and the one born in 1980 has 82 movies.
8. Franz has fewer CDs than Dale, but more than Bethenny.

	Bethenny	Craig	Dale	Elizabeth	Franz	Georgia
Birth Year	1978	1978	1978	1978	1978	1978
	1980	1980	1980	1980	1980	1980
	1982	1982	1982	1982	1982	1982
	1986	1986	1986	1986	1986	1986
	1988	1988	1988	1988	1988	1988
	1992	1992	1992	1992	1992	1992
Movies	36	36	36	36	36	36
	42	42	42	42	42	42
	56	56	56	56	56	56
	62	62	62	62	62	62
	78	78	78	78	78	78
	82	82	82	82	82	82
Music CDs	78	78	78	78	78	78
	82	82	82	82	82	82
	126	126	126	126	126	126
	164	164	164	164	164	164
	186	186	186	186	186	186
	234	234	234	234	234	234

We're Crazy Over Algebra

At Weluvtolearn School, five students are assigned an algebra problem to solve each week. They may choose "lifelines" (partners) to help them solve their problems. Last week, three girls (Ellen, Jillian, and Tawny) and two boys (Frank and Winston) were each assigned a different problem. Each one chose a classmate to provide assistance. Solve the algebra problems (n is the unknown number). As you read the clues, discover who worked as pairs and the answer they got for their problem.

$2n + 7 = 3n - 1$	$n =$ _____
$4n - 5 = 3n - 2$	$n =$ _____
$5n - 9 = 3n + 3$	$n =$ _____
$4n + 6 = 6n - 4$	$n =$ _____
$3n + 5 = 2n + 6$	$n =$ _____

Clues:

1. Jillian chose Hakeem, but did not have the problem $2n + 7 = 3n - 1$ or $4n - 5 = 3n - 2$.
2. One boy chose Lia to help him solve the problem $5n - 9 = 3n + 3$.
3. Frank did not solve $4n - 5 = 3n - 2$.
4. No student's first name and answer began with the same letter.
5. The girl who solved $4n + 6 = 6n - 4$ did not choose Seeley.
6. Of five different students, there was Frank, the girl who chose Fiona, the one who found $n = 8$, Tawny, and the one who solved $3n + 5 = 2n + 6$ with Hakeem.

Ellen	Frank	Jillian	Tawny	Winston
Bradford	Bradford	Bradford	Bradford	Bradford
Fiona	Fiona	Fiona	Fiona	Fiona
Hakeem	Hakeem	Hakeem	Hakeem	Hakeem
Lia	Lia	Lia	Lia	Lia
Seeley	Seeley	Seeley	Seeley	Seeley
$n = 1$	$n = 1$	$n = 1$	$n = 1$	$n = 1$
$n = 3$	$n = 3$	$n = 3$	$n = 3$	$n = 3$
$n = 5$	$n = 5$	$n = 5$	$n = 5$	$n = 5$
$n = 6$	$n = 6$	$n = 6$	$n = 6$	$n = 6$
$n = 8$	$n = 8$	$n = 8$	$n = 8$	$n = 8$

Spice It Up

In the new reality TV show called *Spice It Up*, contestants compete for top honors. Next week's show will feature four spicy contestants who will share their secret recipes. Each will use different amounts of the same three spices: pepper, chives, and mustard. Use the clues to match each contestant with the amount of spices in his or her recipe. First, convert the given amounts to ounces. Remember that 1 Tablespoon (Tbsp) = 3 teaspoons (tsp), 2 Tbsp = 1 ounce (oz), and 1 cup (c) = 8 oz. Write the correct number of oz in the empty spaces. (Three are done for you.) Check solutions to see that your calculations are correct.

Clues:

1. Rosemary uses six times more mustard than Myrtle uses pepper.
2. Rosemary's recipe calls for six times more mustard than Ginger's calls for chives.
3. Basil uses the same amount of pepper as Myrtle uses chives.
4. Ginger's recipe requires six times more mustard than Basil's requires in chives.
5. Ginger uses six times more mustard than Rosemary uses pepper.
6. Ginger's recipe needs $\frac{1}{8}$ oz more chives than are needed in Rosemary's recipe.
7. Basil's recipe uses $\frac{1}{2}$ oz more mustard than Rosemary's does.

	Basil		Ginger		Myrtle		Rosemary	
Pepper	1 tsp	___ oz	1 tsp	___ oz	1 tsp	___ oz	1 tsp	___ oz
	1 ½ tsp	___ oz	1 ½ tsp	___ oz	1 ½ tsp	___ oz	1 ½ tsp	___ oz
	2 tsp	___ oz	2 tsp	___ oz	2 tsp	___ oz	2 tsp	___ oz
	2 ½ tsp	$\frac{5}{12}$ oz	2 ½ tsp	$\frac{5}{12}$ oz	2 ½ tsp	$\frac{5}{12}$ oz	2 ½ tsp	$\frac{5}{12}$ oz
Chives	¼ Tbsp	___ oz	¼ Tbsp	___ oz	¼ Tbsp	___ oz	¼ Tbsp	___ oz
	⅓ Tbsp	___ oz	⅓ Tbsp	___ oz	⅓ Tbsp	___ oz	⅓ Tbsp	___ oz
	½ Tbsp	___ oz	½ Tbsp	___ oz	½ Tbsp	___ oz	½ Tbsp	___ oz
	⅔ Tbsp	$\frac{1}{3}$ oz	⅔ Tbsp	$\frac{1}{3}$ oz	⅔ Tbsp	$\frac{1}{3}$ oz	⅔ Tbsp	$\frac{1}{3}$ oz
Mustard	$\frac{1}{16}$ c	___ oz	$\frac{1}{16}$ c	___ oz	$\frac{1}{16}$ c	___ oz	$\frac{1}{16}$ c	___ oz
	⅛ c	___ oz	⅛ c	___ oz	⅛ c	___ oz	⅛ c	___ oz
	$\frac{3}{16}$ c	___ oz	$\frac{3}{16}$ c	___ oz	$\frac{3}{16}$ c	___ oz	$\frac{3}{16}$ c	___ oz
	¼ c	2 oz	¼ c	2 oz	¼ c	2 oz	¼ c	2 oz

DOI: 10.4324/9781003236382-17

Got Feet?

Four kids (two girls named Hester and Keysha, and two boys named Dex and Millard) went rummaging through their father's woodworking shop to find building materials for a project. Each child collected a piece of board, a length of string, some old garden hose, and some rope. Use the clues to determine the length of each material that each child planned to use. For this puzzle, it will be helpful to complete the conversion chart before beginning. Some have already been filled in for you.

1 rod = 5 ½ yd = 16 ½ ft = 198 in.
1 yd = 3 ft = 36 in.
1 ft = ⅓ yd = 12 in.

Conversion Chart

	Inches	Feet	Yards	Rods
Board	15	1 ¼	⁵⁄₁₂	³⁄₄₀
	27			
	54			
	72			
String	30	2 ½	⅚	⁵⁄₃₃
		5		
		8 ¼		
		11		
Hose	72	6	2	⁴⁄₁₁
			3 ½	
			5	
			8 ¼	
Rope	396	33	11	2
				2 ⅔
				5
				6 ⅓

Got Feet, continued

(Hint: This puzzle is easier to solve if you pay close attention to Clue 1 and Clue 2 as you go. For Clue 1, as soon as you know who had the certain length of board, you should circle the same length of hose for that person. And for Clue 2, as soon as you know who had the longest string, you can also circle the longest hose.)

Clues:

1. One girl had the same lengths of board and garden hose.
2. One of the boys had the longest string and the longest garden hose.
3. Either Keysha's string was half as long as Hester's string, or Keysha's board was half as long as Hester's board.
4. Either Hester's string was twice the length of Millard's string, or Hester's board was twice the length of Millard's board.
5. The one who had a garden hose 3 ½ yd long had a 15-in. board.
6. Keysha's rope was four times the length of Millard's string.
7. Dex's rope was 2 ½ times longer than Millard's rope.

		Dex	Hester	Keysha	Millard
Inches of Board		15 in.	15 in.	15 in.	15 in.
		27 in.	27 in.	27 in.	27 in.
		54 in.	54 in.	54 in.	54 in.
		72 in.	72 in.	72 in.	72 in.
Feet of String		2 ½ ft	2 ½ ft	2 ½ ft	2 ½ ft
		5 ft	5 ft	5 ft	5 ft
		8 ¼ ft	8 ¼ ft	8 ¼ ft	8 ¼ ft
		11 ft	11 ft	11 ft	11 ft
Yards of Hose		2 yd	2 yd	2 yd	2 yd
		3 ½ yd	3 ½ yd	3 ½ yd	3 ½ yd
		5 yd	5 yd	5 yd	5 yd
		8 ¼ yd	8 ¼ yd	8 ¼ yd	8 ¼ yd
Rods of Rope		2 rd	2 rd	2 rd	2 rd
		2 ⅔ rd	2 ⅔ rd	2 ⅔ rd	2 ⅔ rd
		5 rd	5 rd	5 rd	5 rd
		6 ⅓ rd	6 ⅓ rd	6 ⅓ rd	6 ⅓ rd

Boys Love Big Toys

Four boys were curious about large machines. Each boy recorded the weight of a particular ship, rail car, and semi on October 5 at 10:05 am. No vehicle was full at the time it was weighed. The fractions in the left column of the chart show how full each vehicle was at 10:05 on October 5. Convert each fraction to a decimal. For example: $\frac{2}{3}$ = 2 ÷ 3, which is .666. Find the weights in lb in the boxes. Match the weight of each ship, rail car, and semi with the boy who monitored it.

Using 1 ton = 2,000 lb, calculate the full weights in lb, and write them on the lines below.

Each full ship weighs 64,000 tons = _____ lb
Each full rail car weighs 100 tons = _____ lb
Each full semi weighs 27 tons = _____ lb

Clues:

1. The one whose semi was $\frac{7}{8}$ full also had the ship that weighed 80,000,000 lb.
2. Marquette did not have any vehicles $\frac{3}{4}$ full, but Duluth had two that were $\frac{3}{4}$ full.
3. The one who monitored the rail car that weighed 125,000 lb also had the ship that was $\frac{4}{5}$ full.
4. Beaumont's ship weighed 500 times more than Marquette's railcar.
5. Trenton's ship was heavier than Duluth's, and Trenton's semi was heavier than Duluth's.
6. Beaumont's rail car weighed less than the one tracked by the boy whose semi was $\frac{3}{4}$ full.

Boys Love Big Toys, continued

		Beaumont	Duluth	Marquette	Trenton
Ship	⅞ full	112,000,000 lb	112,000,000 lb	112,000,000 lb	112,000,000 lb
	⅘ full	102,400,000 lb	102,400,000 lb	102,400,000 lb	102,400,000 lb
	¾ full	96,000,000 lb	96,000,000 lb	96,000,000 lb	96,000,000 lb
	⅝ full	80,000,000 lb	80,000,000 lb	80,000,000 lb	80,000,000 lb
Rail Car	⅞ full	175,000 lb	175,000 lb	175,000 lb	175,000 lb
	⅘ full	160,000 lb	160,000 lb	160,000 lb	160,000 lb
	¾ full	150,000 lb	150,000 lb	150,000 lb	150,000 lb
	⅝ full	125,000 lb	125,000 lb	125,000 lb	125,000 lb
Semi	⅞ full	47,250 lb	47,250 lb	47,250 lb	47,250 lb
	⅘ full	43,200 lb	43,200 lb	43,200 lb	43,200 lb
	¾ full	40,500 lb	40,500 lb	40,500 lb	40,500 lb
	⅝ full	33,750 lb	33,750 lb	33,750 lb	33,750 lb

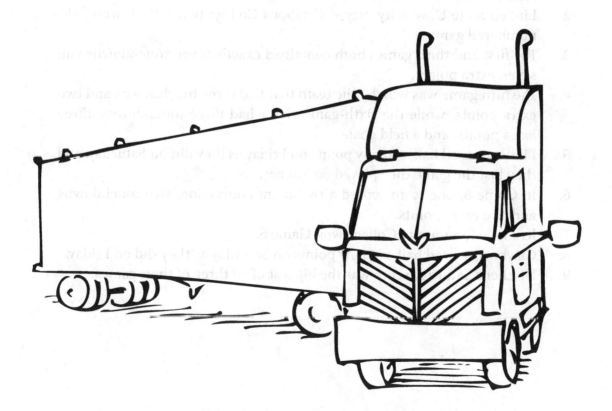

Pigskin Playoffs

Four football teams in areas near each other held a spring training skirmish. Two randomly paired teams played on Friday, two others played on Saturday, and two others played on Sunday. For scoring, a touchdown counted as 6 points, an extra point was 1 point, a two-point conversion was 2 points, and a field goal was 3 points. In the Game column, write 1, 2, 3, 4, 5, or 6 beside the correct score as you determine which game each team played. For example, in Game 2, one team scored 31 points.

Which team scored 31 points in Game 2? _____

Use the scoring information and clues to discover which teams played Games 1 and 2 on Friday, Games 3 and 4 on Saturday, and Games 5 and 6 on Sunday, as well as the number of points each team scored during each of its three games.

Clues:

1. Discher made a field goal, four touchdowns, and four extra points to win Friday's game.
2. Linden State University played Clayborn College twice. Both were odd-numbered games.
3. The first and third games both contained exactly seven touchdowns and seven extra points.
4. The fifth game was won by the team that had three touchdowns and two extra points, while the sixth-game victor had three touchdowns, three extra points, and a field goal.
5. Linden scored half as many points on Friday as they did on Saturday, and they lost the game they played on Sunday.
6. In Game 6, one team scored a two-point conversion, two touchdowns, and two extra points.
7. Kremer Community College won Game 6.
8. Clayborn scored half as many points on Saturday as they did on Friday.
9. Discher's Saturday score was the highest of all three of their games.

Pigskin Playoffs, continued

	Game	Clayborn College	Discher University	Kremer Comm. College	Linden State University
Friday **Games** **1 and 2**	2	21 28 30 31	21 28 30 31	21 28 30 31	21 28 30 31
Saturday **Games** **3 and 4**		14 27 35 42	14 27 35 42	14 27 35 42	14 27 35 42
Sunday **Games** **5 and 6**		16 17 20 24	16 17 20 24	16 17 20 24	16 17 20 24

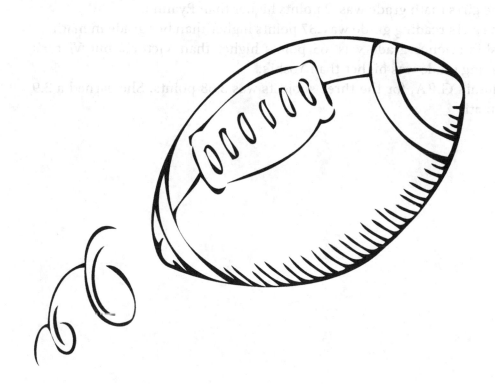

What's My G.P.A.?

Five classmates (three girls named Ryann, Salomi, and Yoshi, and two boys named Pearce and Victor) just received their excellent semester report cards. They compared grades for three subjects: math, science, and reading. An A average is 4.0 points, a B average is 3.0 points, a C average is 2.0 points, and so on. Decimals are used for grades that fall between these numbers. Use the clues to find out what grade each student received in each of the three subjects. To solve this puzzle, you will need to calculate each student's grade point average (G.P.A.). Add the three decimals for each of his or her three subject scores, and then divide by three.

Whose G.P.A. was highest? _____

Clues:

1. Pearce had a higher grade in math than Victor by .2 points.
2. One girl's reading grade was .045 points higher than her science grade.
3. One boy's science grade was .175 points lower than Salomi's and .3 higher than Ryann's.
4. One girl's math grade was .2 points higher than Ryann's.
5. One girl's reading grade was .37 points higher than her grade in math.
6. Yoshi's science grade was .65 points higher than Victor's, but Victor's reading grade was higher than Yoshi's.
7. Salomi's G.P.A. for the three subjects was 3.68 points. She earned a 3.9 in math.

DOI: 10.4324/9781003236382-21

	Pearce	Ryann	Salomi	Victor	Yoshi
	G.P.A.	G.P.A.	G.P.A.	G.P.A.	G.P.A.
Math	3.2	3.2	3.2	3.2	3.2
	3.4	3.4	3.4	3.4	3.4
	3.55	3.55	3.55	3.55	3.55
	3.75	3.75	3.75	3.75	3.75
	3.9	3.9	3.9	3.9	3.9
Science	2.875	2.875	2.875	2.875	2.875
	3.175	3.175	3.175	3.175	3.175
	3.35	3.35	3.35	3.35	3.35
	3.65	3.65	3.65	3.65	3.65
	3.825	3.825	3.825	3.825	3.825
Reading	3.74	3.74	3.74	3.74	3.74
	3.79	3.79	3.79	3.79	3.79
	3.87	3.87	3.87	3.87	3.87
	3.92	3.92	3.92	3.92	3.92
	4.0	4.0	4.0	4.0	4.0

Name:.. Date:...................................

Four students in Ms. Farnham's math class played a game in which each student drew cards with single, squared, cubed, and biquadratic numbers on them. Students recalled what they knew about raising numbers to the second, third, and fourth powers as they calculated the outcomes.

A squared number (n^2) is n x n.
A cubed number (n^3) is n x n x n.
A biquadratic number (n^4) is n x n x n x n.

Calculate the squared, cubed, and biquadratic numbers for 2, 3, 4, and 5. Write these in the columns. For example, 7 x 7 = 49 (squared); 7 x 7 x 7 = 343 (cubed); and 7 x 7 x 7 x 7 = 2,401 (biquadratic). Then use the clues to determine which four cards each student drew.

Clues:

1. Karyl's single and cubed numbers were smaller than Richard's, but her square was larger than Richard's.
2. Karyl's single number times Donna's square equaled Jeff's cube.
3. Jeff's single number, square, and biquadratic number were all smaller than Karyl's.
4. Donna's single number times Jeff's square equaled Richard's cube.
5. Jeff's biquadratic number, when squared, equaled Richard's biquadratic number.
6. Jeff had the same number on two different cards.
7. Richard's single number times Donna's cube equaled Karyl's biquadratic number.

Don't Freeze These Cubes, continued

		Donna	Jeff	Karyl	Richard
Single n	2 3 4 5	2 3 4 5	2 3 4 5	2 3 4 5	2 3 4 5
Squared n^2	2 x 2 3 x 3 4 x 4 5 x 5				
Cubed n^3	2 x 2 x 2 3 x 3 x 3 4 x 4 x 4 5 x 5 x 5				
Biquadratic n^4	2 x 2 x 2 x 2 3 x 3 x 3 x 3 4 x 4 x 4 x 4 5 x 5 x 5 x 5				

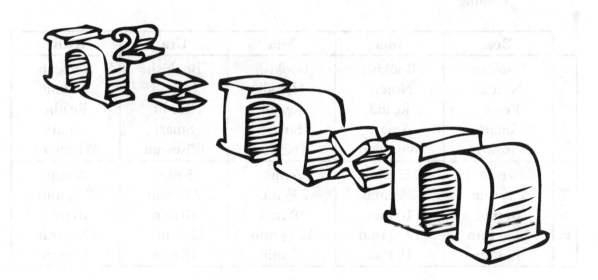

What Did You Call Me?

Five teachers called in sick on the same day. The principal needed to hire substitutes quickly. The three female and two male substitutes all had very strange names—one man had the first name Willie, for instance, and another man had the last name Wisewun. Students were on their best behavior all day, so each substitute gave his or her class a reward. Two substitutes shortened the time period for their subjects, one substitute read to the class for more minutes (min) than scheduled, and two substitutes gave extra time for other activities (a break and lunch). (Hint: It will be helpful to make notes about these schedule changes.) Can you discover each teacher's first and last name, plus the length of the reward he or she gave the class?

Clues:

1. Miss Noitall's reward was either longer lunch or 10 min less of a subject.
2. Mia is not Mrs. Bookish, and Ura is not a woman.
3. Bea taught in the room next to Ms. Smart.
4. Mr. Wisewun did not give 12 ½ min extra in a subject.
5. Mia gave students either a 15 min extra break or 5 min less time in a subject.
6. The male teachers gave 7 ½ min and 12 ½ min longer times as rewards.
7. Neither Ima nor Mrs. Bookish gave students extra break time.
8. Although both classes were reduced, a math test required more time than spelling.

	Bea	Ima	Mia	Ura	Willie
Last Name	Bookish Noitall Readit Smart Wisewun	Bookish Noitall Readit Smart Wisewun	Bookish Noitall Readit Smart Wisewun	Bookish Noitall Readit Smart Wisewun	Bookish Noitall Readit Smart Wisewun
Reward	5 min 7 ½ min 10 min 12 ½ min 15 min	5 min 7 ½ min 10 min 12 ½ min 15 min	5 min 7 ½ min 10 min 12 ½ min 15 min	5 min 7 ½ min 10 min 12 ½ min 15 min	5 min 7 ½ min 10 min 12 ½ min 15 min

I'm a Computer Nut

Students at Savvy Tech School are using various computer programs. Each student logs on using a different password and explores a different program. The three girls (Amata, Bonnie, and Elena) are good friends. The boys (Chris, Damien, and Florian) play baseball together. Can you use the clues to figure out each student's password and which program he or she is using?

Clues:

1. One of the boys whose passwords are mrrogers1928 and fasttyper176 is using PowerPoint. (Mr. Rogers was born in 1928 and is a favorite TV personality of this boy.)
2. Three girls (the one using search engines, her friend whose password is butterfly132, and Amata) are having a party next week.
3. Of six students, there are Damien, Elena, the ones using search engines and the Internet, and the ones whose passwords are yogurt396 and fasttyper176.
4. The girl whose password is yogurt396 is creating a web with Inspiration.
5. None of the boys, nor the girl using Excel, has the password mtdew1948.
6. Chris is not using PowerPoint and does not have mrrogers1928 as his password.
7. The three boys are Chris, the one whose password is fasttyper176, and the one creating a photo collage using Picasa.

Amata	Bonnie	Chris	Damien	Elena	Florian
butterfly132	butterfly132	butterfly132	butterfly132	butterfly132	butterfly132
decoder405	decoder405	decoder405	decoder405	decoder405	decoder405
fasttyper176	fasttyper176	fasttyper176	fasttyper176	fasttyper176	fasttyper176
mrrogers1928	mrrogers1928	mrrogers1928	mrrogers1928	mrrogers1928	mrrogers1928
mtdew1948	mtdew1948	mtdew1948	mtdew1948	mtdew1948	mtdew1948
yogurt396	yogurt396	yogurt396	yogurt396	yogurt396	yogurt396
Excel	Excel	Excel	Excel	Excel	Excel
Inspiration	Inspiration	Inspiration	Inspiration	Inspiration	Inspiration
Internet	Internet	Internet	Internet	Internet	Internet
Picasa	Picasa	Picasa	Picasa	Picasa	Picasa
PowerPoint	PowerPoint	PowerPoint	PowerPoint	PowerPoint	PowerPoint
search engine	search engine	search engine	search engine	search engine	search engine

Got My Numbers?

Five girls met at camp last summer and became friends. They live in different states, but they still stay in touch. Each girl is a different age and has a different phone number and address. Use the clues to learn each girl's age, phone number, and house number. You will need to do some calculations for this puzzle. First, add the seven digits for each phone number. (For example, for the phone number 316-4067, 3 + 1 + 6 + 4 + 0 + 6 + 7 = 27.) Write each sum in the empty box beside the number. Next, find factors less than 12 for each four-digit house number. Write the factor in the empty box beside the house number. (Hint: It is necessary to pay close attention to the details in the clues, apply information from previous clues, use syllogistic thinking, and write notes in the margin—one of these has been done for you as an example.)

Clues:

1. Delynn's phone number digits add up to 30.
2. Carissa and Emily are either 13 or 14 years old.
3. Abrah's and Emily's phone numbers' digits total either 27 or 37.
4. The girl whose phone number's digits add up to 30 is 15 years old.
5. The 13-year-old lives at a house number that is divisible by 7.
6. The girl who lives at house number 1203 is 17 years old.
7. Abrah's house number is divisible by 5, and her phone number's digits add up to 27.
8. The 14-year-old lives at a house number that is divisible by 11.
9. The one whose phone number's digits sum to 32 lives in house number 1331.

DOI: 10.4324/9781003236382-25

Got My Numbers?, continued

	Abrah	Carissa	Delynn	Emily	Whitney	Notes
▼ Numbers	13 years	13 years	13 years	13 years	13 years	
	14 years	14 years	14 years	14 years	14 years	
	15 years	15 years	15 years	15 years	15 years	
	16 years	16 years	16 years	16 years	16 years	
	17 years	17 years	17 years	17 years	17 years	
	316-4067	316-4067	316-4067	316-4067	316-4067	
	526-1439	526-1439	526-1439	526-1439	526-1439	
	815-1593	815-1593	815-1593	815-1593	815-1593	
	472-6951	472-6951	472-6951	472-6951	472-6951	
	942-6538	942-6538	942-6538	942-6538	942-6538	
	1203	1203	1203	1203	1203	
	1331	1331	1331	1331	1331	phone is 32
	3437	3437	3437	3437	3437	
	4985	4985	4985	4985	4985	
	6416	6416	6416	6416	6416	

Four children who enjoy solving Sudoku puzzles hold a contest to see who can be the first to solve the same three Sudoku puzzles. In Sudoku, players fill a 9 x 9 grid with digits so that each column, row, and 3 x 3 sub-grid (there are nine) that make up the big grid contains the digits 1–9. Therefore, each digit from 1 to 9 appears nine times in the puzzle. Each child solves all three puzzles correctly, but in different number order, and each child keeps track of which number he or she places all nine of first in each puzzle. No child places the

7			6			2		
	3	2	9	7	5			
	6	5		4	3			
	6	8			7	1		
1		7			9			5
	9	5			2	8		
	4	8		2	1			
	1	3	5	6	4			
5			1			3		

Sample Sudoku Grid

same number first in any of the three puzzles. (Hint: This means that if someone places all of the 8s first in Puzzle 1, then you can cross out 8 for the other two puzzles, and so on.) Determine which number each child places first in each of the three puzzles.

Clues:

1. Debra's, Ramon's, and Underwood's first-placed numbers in Puzzle 2 are larger than their numbers in Puzzle 1, but smaller than their numbers in Puzzle 3.
2. Out of four players, there is Ramon, the one who places 5 first in Puzzle 2, the one who places 6 first in Puzzle 3, and the one who places 4 first in Puzzle 1.
3. The one who places 4 first in Puzzle 1 places 7 first in Puzzle 2, but does not place 9 first in Puzzle 3.
4. In Puzzle 2, Ramon's first-placed number is larger than Maria's.
5. Debra's first-placed number is smaller than Underwood's in both Puzzle 1 and Puzzle 2.

Sudoku Solutions, continued

	Debra	Maria	Ramon	Underwood
Puzzle 1	1 3 4 8	1 3 4 8	1 3 4 8	1 3 4 8
Puzzle 2	2 3 5 7	2 3 5 7	2 3 5 7	2 3 5 7
Puzzle 3	4 6 8 9	4 6 8 9	4 6 8 9	4 6 8 9

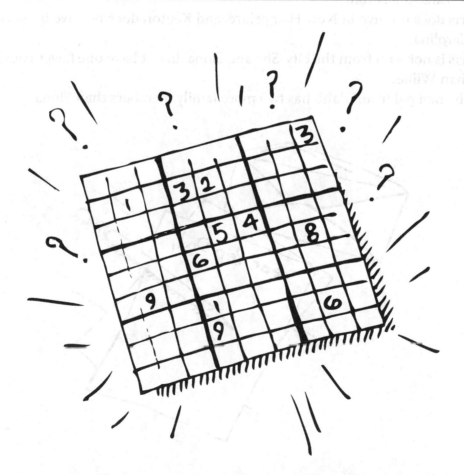

Pen Pal Pursuits

Five pen pals e-mail one another about their families. Use the clues to find out how many family members and cousins each has, and how far each lives from his or her capital city. Convert the number of feet to miles (5,280 ft = 1 mi), and write the miles as decimals in the columns.

Clues:

1. Fiona lives in Kansas. She is not the one who has three fewer cousins than Willie.
2. Neither Kenton nor Willie lives in Idaho or New Hampshire, neither has three or five family members, and neither lives as far from a capital city as Darrion.
3. The one with five family members (one fewer than Willie) lives 4 miles from a capital city.
4. Kenton lives twice as far from a capital city as Willie, Willie has twice as many family members as Darrion, and Darrion has twice as many cousins as Kenton.
5. Iris does not live in New Hampshire, and Kenton does not live in North Carolina.
6. Iris is not 4 mi from the city. She and Fiona do not have one fewer cousin than Willie.
7. The pen pal from Idaho has two more family members than Fiona.

Pen Pal Pursuits, continued

	Darrion	Fiona	Iris	Kenton	Willie
Number of Family Members	3 members 4 members 5 members 6 members 7 members	3 members 4 members 5 members 6 members 7 members	3 members 4 members 5 members 6 members 7 members	3 members 4 members 5 members 6 members 7 members	3 members 4 members 5 members 6 members 7 members
Number of Cousins	4 cousins 6 cousins 8 cousins 9 cousins 12 cousins	4 cousins 6 cousins 8 cousins 9 cousins 12 cousins	4 cousins 6 cousins 8 cousins 9 cousins 12 cousins	4 cousins 6 cousins 8 cousins 9 cousins 12 cousins	4 cousins 6 cousins 8 cousins 9 cousins 12 cousins
17,160 ft **21,120 ft** **30,360 ft** **34,320 ft** **45,408 ft**	_____ mi _____ mi _____ mi _____ mi _____ mi	_____ mi _____ mi _____ mi _____ mi _____ mi	_____ mi _____ mi _____ mi _____ mi _____ mi	_____ mi _____ mi _____ mi _____ mi _____ mi	_____ mi _____ mi _____ mi _____ mi _____ mi
Capital City	Boise, ID Concord, NH Hartford, CT Raleigh, NC Topeka, KS	Boise, ID Concord, NH Hartford, CT Raleigh, NC Topeka, KS	Boise, ID Concord, NH Hartford, CT Raleigh, NC Topeka, KS	Boise, ID Concord, NH Hartford, CT Raleigh, NC Topeka, KS	Boise, ID Concord, NH Hartford, CT Raleigh, NC Topeka, KS

Which Will Be My Alma Mater?

Four students searched the Internet for the cost of attending college. They researched Colorado State University, Columbia University, St. Olaf College, and Washington State University. In addition to an academic program and a campus culture that are good fits, each student must consider scholarships and financial aid, as well as each school's costs of tuition, room and board, books, and other expenses. Use the clues to match each student with his or her dream college and to find the various estimated costs that each student can anticipate. Under the student's name, write the college or university that he or she is considering.

Clues:

1. Tuition and fees plus room and board cost $19,152 at Washington State and $53,874 at Columbia.
2. The estimated cost for books and supplies at Noriko's choice of college is $2,807.
3. Faithe would need less than Jamaal for both personal expenses and books and supplies.
4. St. Olaf's tuition and fees would be about $13,000 more than tuition and fees at the college Jamaal is considering.
5. Neither Noriko nor Jamaal anticipates spending $9,664 on room and board.
6. One student would spend $100 more on books and supplies than on personal expenses.
7. Noriko's room and board would be about five times more than Kipling's personal expenses.
8. Jamaal would spend nearly $600 more than Faithe on room and board and nearly $900 more than Noriko on personal expenses.

Which Will Be My Alma Mater?, continued

College ▶	Faithe	Jamaal	Kipling	Noriko
Tuition and Fees	$9,488 $23,096 $36,800 $43,304	$9,488 $23,096 $36,800 $43,304	$9,488 $23,096 $36,800 $43,304	$9,488 $23,096 $36,800 $43,304
Room and Board	$8,500 $9,084 $9,664 $10,570	$8,500 $9,084 $9,664 $10,570	$8,500 $9,084 $9,664 $10,570	$8,500 $9,084 $9,664 $10,570
Books and Supplies	$936 $1,000 $1,126 $2,807	$936 $1,000 $1,126 $2,807	$936 $1,000 $1,126 $2,807	$936 $1,000 $1,126 $2,807
Personal Expenses	$900 $1,500 $2,108 $2,392	$900 $1,500 $2,108 $2,392	$900 $1,500 $2,108 $2,392	$900 $1,500 $2,108 $2,392

What's My Total?

Four friends headed to the shopping mall to choose gifts for their moms for Mother's Day. They totally confused the poor clerk, who got mixed up by their names! Each boy chose a different item of a different price, received a different percent discount, and paid a different total amount. You will need to make notes of the items beside names and prices in order to solve this puzzle. Use the clues to find each boy's first and last name (nobody's first name is the same as his last name), the item he bought, its original price, and the discount. Then calculate the total cost by subtracting the discount. (To calculate the total price, multiply the original price by the decimal discount, and then subtract the discount amount from the original price.)

> **Example:**
> For a 25% discount on a $10 item, $10 x .25 = 2.5, and $10 – 2.5 = $7.50 total.

Clues:

1. Burke's last name comes alphabetically earlier than Chandler's.
2. Andrew got 15% off the original price of the perfume, while the boy whose last name is Wallace got a 12% discount.
3. The boy whose last name is Chandler chose a picture frame for $8.50, and Wallace's floral bouquet cost $8.00.
4. One boy bought a candle for $9.50, while another got 10% off a bouquet of flowers.

What's My Total?, continued

	Andrew	Burke	Chandler	Wallace
Last Name	Andrew Burke Chandler Wallace	Andrew Burke Chandler Wallace	Andrew Burke Chandler Wallace	Andrew Burke Chandler Wallace
Original Price	$8.00 $8.50 $9.00 $9.50	$8.00 $8.50 $9.00 $9.50	$8.00 $8.50 $9.00 $9.50	$8.00 $8.50 $9.00 $9.50
Percent Discount	8% 10% 12% 15%	8% 10% 12% 15%	8% 10% 12% 15%	8% 10% 12% 15%
Total Price	$7.20 $7.65 $7.82 $8.36	$7.20 $7.65 $7.82 $8.36	$7.20 $7.65 $7.82 $8.36	$7.20 $7.65 $7.82 $8.36

Our Loyal Fans

Have you ever heard the saying "It's as American as Mom, baseball, and apple pie?" Americans love watching and attending baseball games to cheer for their favorite teams, hoping to see them play in the World Series, such as the Rangers and the Giants did in 2010. The total attendance numbers for six major-league baseball teams are listed below, along with each team's home average attendance and road average attendance. See if you can bat 1,000 at fielding the clues to determine each team's attendance during the 2010 season.

Clues:

1. The Cubs' home average was less than the Cardinals' but higher than the Rangers' and the Red Sox's.
2. The Yankees had 464,589 more in total attendance than the Cardinals.
3. The Red Sox had fewer total fans attending games than the Cubs.
4. The Giants' road average was 237 lower than the Cubs'.
5. The difference between the Red Sox's home and road averages was 5,325.
6. One team's road average (30,687) was about 10,000 less than its home average (40,755).
7. The two 2010 World Series teams had the lowest total attendance of these six teams.
8. The Cardinals' road average was higher than the Rangers' but lower than the Yankees'.
9. One team had the highest total attendance and home average, while the Rangers had the lowest.

Our Loyal Fans, continued

		St. Louis Cardinals	Chicago Cubs	San Fran. Giants	Texas Rangers	Boston Red Sox	New York Yankees
Total Attendance		2,505,171	2,505,171	2,505,171	2,505,171	2,505,171	2,505,171
		3,037,443	3,037,443	3,037,443	3,037,443	3,037,443	3,037,443
		3,046,445	3,046,445	3,046,445	3,046,445	3,046,445	3,046,445
		3,062,973	3,062,973	3,062,973	3,062,973	3,062,973	3,062,973
		3,301,218	3,301,218	3,301,218	3,301,218	3,301,218	3,301,218
		3,765,807	3,765,807	3,765,807	3,765,807	3,765,807	3,765,807
Road Average		26,565	26,565	26,565	26,565	26,565	26,565
		30,687	30,687	30,687	30,687	30,687	30,687
		32,035	32,035	32,035	32,035	32,035	32,035
		32,272	32,272	32,272	32,272	32,272	32,272
		32,285	32,285	32,285	32,285	32,285	32,285
		34,939	34,939	34,939	34,939	34,939	34,939
Home Average		30,385	30,385	30,385	30,385	30,385	30,385
		37,499	37,499	37,499	37,499	37,499	37,499
		37,610	37,610	37,610	37,610	37,610	37,610
		37,814	37,814	37,814	37,814	37,814	37,814
		40,755	40,755	40,755	40,755	40,755	40,755
		46,491	46,491	46,491	46,491	46,491	46,491

The Bouncing Bartletts

The Bartlett kids are very active. The girls (Elicia and Phaedra) like to plan family contests in hopping, pogo stick jumping, and jogging. Convert each amount as indicated. Write the amounts for miles (mi), yards (yd), and feet (ft) in the column. Discover the age of each child and the distances each one jogged, jumped, and hopped. (Hint: This puzzle will be easier to solve if you refer back to previous clues as you go.)

1,760 yd = 1 mi (to find mi from given yd, divide yd by 1760)
3 ft = 1 yd (to find yd from given ft, divide ft by 3)
12 in. = 1 ft (to find ft from given in., divide in. by 12)

Clues:

1. Elicia jogged ⅛ mi less than Terrence.
2. The one who hopped 15 ft jumped 15 yd.
3. Nolan is ⅓ as old as Kyzer, and Elicia is ⅓ as old as Terrence.
4. The 6-year-old hopped 1 ft less than she jumped.
5. Kyzer and Phaedra both hopped ⅑ as far as they jumped.
6. The 15-year-old jogged ⅗ mi, which is 88 times as many yd as he jumped.
7. The 18 year old jogged ¼ mi and jumped half as far as Kyzer.
8. Nolan jogged farther than the 10-year-old.

DOI: 10.4324/9781003236382-31

Bouncing Bartletts, continued

		Elicia	Kyzer	Nolan	Phaedra	Terrence
Jogging	_____ mi	220 yd	220 yd	220 yd	220 yd	220 yd
	_____ mi	352 yd	352 yd	352 yd	352 yd	352 yd
	_____ mi	440 yd	440 yd	440 yd	440 yd	440 yd
	_____ mi	660 yd	660 yd	660 yd	660 yd	660 yd
	_____ mi	1,056 yd	1,056 yd	1,056 yd	1,056 yd	1,056 yd
Jumping	_____ yd	12 ft	12 ft	12 ft	12 ft	12 ft
	_____ yd	18 ft	18 ft	18 ft	18 ft	18 ft
	_____ yd	27 ft	27 ft	27 ft	27 ft	27 ft
	_____ yd	36 ft	36 ft	36 ft	36 ft	36 ft
	_____ yd	45 ft	45 ft	45 ft	45 ft	45 ft
Hopping	_____ ft	36 in.	36 in.	36 in.	36 in.	36 in.
	_____ ft	48 in.	48 in.	48 in.	48 in.	48 in.
	_____ ft	84 in.	84 in.	84 in.	84 in.	84 in.
	_____ ft	132 in.	132 in.	132 in.	132 in.	132 in.
	_____ ft	180 in.	180 in.	180 in.	180 in.	180 in.
Age		5	5	5	5	5
		6	6	6	6	6
		10	10	10	10	10
		15	15	15	15	15
		18	18	18	18	18

Shape Up: Double Workout (Part I)

During geometry class, Mr. Barber handed five students each a different regular polygon and asked them to name their polygons. Three named their shapes correctly, but two did not. The class reviewed the following: five sides = pentagon, six sides = hexagon, seven sides = heptagon, eight sides = octagon, and nine sides = nonagon. Next, Mr. Barber asked those five students each to choose one shape and measure its sides. It was time to learn about perimeter. Use the clues to find out how many sides each student's assigned shape (the one he or she was asked about) had and what he or she called it. Then find out the side length of the shape that each student chose to measure.

Clues:

1. One student correctly named his assigned shape as a nonagon, but that was not the shape he chose to measure. The shape he measured had 2.2-cm sides.
2. One student chose to measure the seven sides of his or her shape and found that they were 1.9 cm, but incorrectly named the shape an octagon.
3. Enola was not asked about the six-sided shape by Mr. Barber.
4. Darshan and Seth named their shapes heptagon and nonagon when called on, but only one of them—the one asked about the nonagon—was correct.
5. Lani was asked about a shape with five sides. She did not name it hexagon or octagon.
6. Darshan said that his eight-sided figure was a heptagon. That was incorrect.
7. Darshan did not measure 2.8 cm as the length of the sides on his chosen shape.
8. Lani measured the sides of her chosen shape as 1.5 cm, but it was not the shape she was asked about in class.
9. Seth knew the name of the nine-sided shape he was asked about.

DOI: 10.4324/9781003236382-32

Shape Up Part 1, continued

	Darshan	Enola	Lani	Seth	Tierra
Number of Sides on Assigned Shape	five six seven eight nine	five six seven eight nine	five six seven eight nine	five six seven eight nine	five six seven eight nine
Name Guessed for Assigned Shape	pentagon hexagon heptagon octagon nonagon	pentagon hexagon heptagon octagon nonagon	pentagon hexagon heptagon octagon nonagon	pentagon hexagon heptagon octagon nonagon	pentagon hexagon heptagon octagon nonagon
Length of Sides of Chosen Shape	1.5 cm 1.8 cm 1.9 cm 2.2 cm 2.8 cm	1.5 cm 1.8 cm 1.9 cm 2.2 cm 2.8 cm	1.5 cm 1.8 cm 1.9 cm 2.2 cm 2.8 cm	1.5 cm 1.8 cm 1.9 cm 2.2 cm 2.8 cm	1.5 cm 1.8 cm 1.9 cm 2.2 cm 2.8 cm

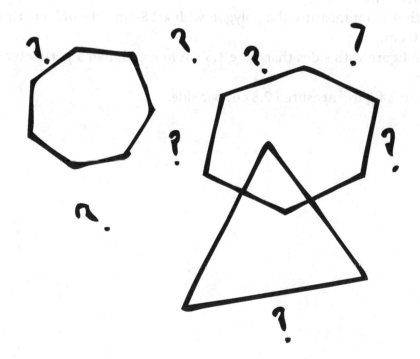

Shape Up: Double Workout (Part II)

Mr. Barber asked five students to choose a regular (equilateral) polygon, measure its sides, and calculate its perimeter. Only Enola and Darshan chose the same shape that they were originally assigned. Use Part I to recall assigned shapes. Find out the number of sides each student's chosen shape had, the length of the sides he or she measured, and the perimeter of each one's chosen shape. It may seem as if there are not enough clues. You will need to do some deep thinking and some calculations to figure it all out. The formula for the perimeter of an equilateral polygon is n x a (where *n* is the number of sides, and *a* is the length of one side).

Example:
For a square with 2.1-cm sides, there are 4 sides x 2.1 cm length = 8.4 cm perimeter
Perimeter is 8.4 cm ÷ 4 sides = 2.1-cm length
Perimeter is 8.4 cm ÷ 2.1-cm length = 4 sides

Clues:

1. One student measured a side of the nonagon and calculated its perimeter at 13.5 cm.
2. Seth did not measure the polygon with a 2.8-cm side and a perimeter of 14.0 cm.
3. The figure with sides that were 1.8 cm in length had a perimeter of 14.4 cm.
4. Tierra's figure measured 2.8 cm per side.

Shape Up Part II, continued

	Darshan	Enola	Lani	Seth	Tierra
Number of Sides Measured	five six seven eight nine	five six seven eight nine	five six seven eight nine	five six seven eight nine	five six seven eight nine
Length of Sides Measured	1.5 cm 1.8 cm 1.9 cm 2.2 cm 2.8 cm	1.5 cm 1.8 cm 1.9 cm 2.2 cm 2.8 cm	1.5 cm 1.8 cm 1.9 cm 2.2 cm 2.8 cm	1.5 cm 1.8 cm 1.9 cm 2.2 cm 2.8 cm	1.5 cm 1.8 cm 1.9 cm 2.2 cm 2.8 cm
Perimeter	13.2 cm 13.3 cm 13.5 cm 14.0 cm 14.4 cm	13.2 cm 13.3 cm 13.5 cm 14.0 cm 14.4 cm	13.2 cm 13.3 cm 13.5 cm 14.0 cm 14.4 cm	13.2 cm 13.3 cm 13.5 cm 14.0 cm 14.4 cm	13.2 cm 13.3 cm 13.5 cm 14.0 cm 14.4 cm

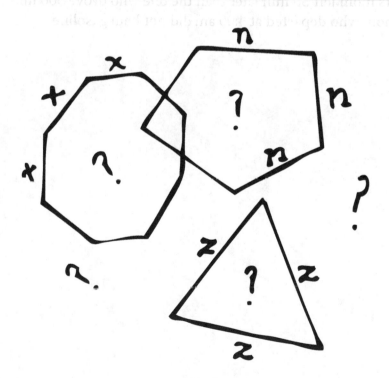

Miles for Moms

Five neighbors have moms who are delivery drivers. Their cargoes vary from day to day, and so does the length of their driving assignments. Last Monday, each mom had a new route that she had never driven before. Use the clues to determine each mom's distance, cargo, and time of day she left to make her delivery. (Hint: It will be necessary to make notes about items that go together but can't be marked anywhere.)

Clues:

1. Graham's mom drove 100 miles (mi). She left 60 minutes (min) earlier than Aiden's mom.
2. The 500-mi driver transported logs, and the 300-mi driver hauled milk.
3. Jackson's mom left 60 min later than the mom who delivered milk.
4. The mom who delivered milk departed 30 min earlier than Graham's mom and 30 min later than the mom who drove 200 mi.
5. The mom whose cargo was bread left 30 min after the mom who carried milk.
6. Carter's mom did not drive 200 or 500 mi, and she did not carry mail or gasoline.
7. Aiden's mom left 30 min later than the one who drove 500 mi.
8. The mom who departed at 4:00 am did not haul gasoline.

DOI: 10.4324/9781003236382-34

Aiden's Mom	Carter's Mom	Elijah's Mom	Graham's Mom	Jackson's Mom
100 mi	100 mi	100 mi	100 mi	100 mi
200 mi	200 mi	200 mi	200 mi	200 mi
300 mi	300 mi	300 mi	300 mi	300 mi
400 mi	400 mi	400 mi	400 mi	400 mi
500 mi	500 mi	500 mi	500 mi	500 mi
bread	bread	bread	bread	bread
gasoline	gasoline	gasoline	gasoline	gasoline
logs	logs	logs	logs	logs
mail	mail	mail	mail	mail
milk	milk	milk	milk	milk
4:00 am	4:00 am	4:00 am	4:00 am	4:00 am
4:30 am	4:30 am	4:30 am	4:30 am	4:30 am
5:00 am	5:00 am	5:00 am	5:00 am	5:00 am
5:30 am	5:30 am	5:30 am	5:30 am	5:30 am
6:00 am	6:00 am	6:00 am	6:00 am	6:00 am

Climb Ev'ry Mountain

Students were learning about elevation during social studies class. They found the following information about five different states: highest point, highest elevation, lowest point, and lowest elevation. Use the clues to determine the facts about each state. Remember that 5,280 feet (ft) = 1 mile (mi). To find the decimal that represents mi above sea level, divide number of ft by 5,280.

State abbreviations: California–CA, Kentucky–KY, Michigan–MI, Montana–MT, South Dakota–SD

Clues:

1. The elevation of Harney Peak, SD, is more than 1 mi, and Bigstone Lake's elevation is 966 ft.
2. The Kootenai River is about ⅓ mi above sea level, and it is not in KY or MI.
3. Death Valley is the nation's lowest elevation. It is only 86 mi from Mt. Whitney and is located in the same state.
4. Black Mountain, KY, is a little over ¾ mi above sea level, while SD's lowest point is 966 ft.
5. Of five different states, there is California, the one with the Kootenai River, the one with 257 ft as its lowest elevation, the one with Harney Peak, and the one with 1,979 ft as its highest elevation.
6. Montana's Granite Peak is more than 2 mi above sea level.
7. At 2 ¾ mi, Mount Whitney, CA, is the highest summit in the 48 contiguous states.
8. The Mississippi River does not border or flow through MI.

Climb Ev'ry Mountain, continued

	CA	KY	MI	MT	SD
Lowest Point	Bigstone Lake Death Valley Kootenai River Lake Erie Mississippi R.	Bigstone Lake Death Valley Kootenai River Lake Erie Mississippi R.	Bigstone Lake Death Valley Kootenai River Lake Erie Mississippi R.	Bigstone Lake Death Valley Kootenai River Lake Erie Mississippi R.	Bigstone Lake Death Valley Kootenai River Lake Erie Mississippi R.
Lowest Elevation	−282 ft 257 ft 572 ft 966 ft 1,800 ft	−282 ft 257 ft 572 ft 966 ft 1,800 ft	−282 ft 257 ft 572 ft 966 ft 1,800 ft	−282 ft 257 ft 572 ft 966 ft 1,800 ft	−282 ft 257 ft 572 ft 966 ft 1,800 ft
Highest Point	Black Mt. Granite Peak Harney Peak Mt. Arvon Mt. Whitney	Black Mt. Granite Peak Harney Peak Mt. Arvon Mt. Whitney	Black Mt. Granite Peak Harney Peak Mt. Arvon Mt. Whitney	Black Mt. Granite Peak Harney Peak Mt. Arvon Mt. Whitney	Black Mt. Granite Peak Harney Peak Mt. Arvon Mt. Whitney
Highest Elevation	1,979 ft 4,139 ft 7,242 ft 12,799 ft 14,494 ft	1,979 ft 4,139 ft 7,242 ft 12,799 ft 14,494 ft	1,979 ft 4,139 ft 7,242 ft 12,799 ft 14,494 ft	1,979 ft 4,139 ft 7,242 ft 12,799 ft 14,494 ft	1,979 ft 4,139 ft 7,242 ft 12,799 ft 14,494 ft

What's Your Number?

Mr. and Mrs. Lentz have two sons and a daughter. They noticed a mathematical phenomenon in their family this year. Add the digits for each family member's age, birthday, and bank account. (For example, the digits for an age of 15 are 1 + 5 = 6; adding the month and day for April 28 gives you 4 + 28 = 32; and the digits for a bank account of 1234-5678 yields 1 + 2 + 3 + 4 + 5 + 6 + 7 + 8 = 36). Three numbers have been entered for you. Write the others in the provided column. Check the numbers in the solutions section in the back to make sure that you are correct. Use the clues and numbers to find each person's age and age number, birthday and birthday number, and bank account and bank account number.

What is the relationship? _____

Clues:

1. Mason's birthday number is not a multiple of 6, but his bank account number is.
2. Thad's bank account number is not a multiple of 6, but his birthday number is.
3. Kirk's age number is a multiple of Ellie's age number, which is the square root of her birthday number.
4. Thad's age number is a factor of his mother's age number.
5. Thad's birthday number is a multiple of his dad's birthday number.
6. Cindy's age number is a factor of Thad's bank account number.
7. Ellie's and Mason's birthday numbers are not factors of Cindy's or Kirk's bank account numbers.
8. Everyone's age number is a factor of his or her birthday number and bank account number. That's the relationship!

DOI: 10.4324/9781003236382-36

	#	Cindy	Ellie	Kirk	Mason	Thad
Age	4	22	22	22	22	22
		23	23	23	23	23
		30	30	30	30	30
		60	60	60	60	60
		62	62	62	62	62
Birthday	12	Feb. 10	Feb. 10	Feb. 10	Feb. 10	Feb. 10
		Mar. 21	Mar. 21	Mar. 21	Mar. 21	Mar. 21
		May 4	May 4	May 4	May 4	May 4
		Aug. 12	Aug. 12	Aug. 12	Aug. 12	Aug. 12
		Oct. 26	Oct. 26	Oct. 26	Oct. 26	Oct. 26
Bank Account	40	5639-7253	5639-7253	5639-7253	5639-7253	5639-7253
		3509-8241	3509-8241	3509-8241	3509-8241	3509-8241
		6201-2016	6201-2016	6201-2016	6201-2016	6201-2016
		2036-5743	2036-5743	2036-5743	2036-5743	2036-5743
		5480-4975	5480-4975	5480-4975	5480-4975	5480-4975

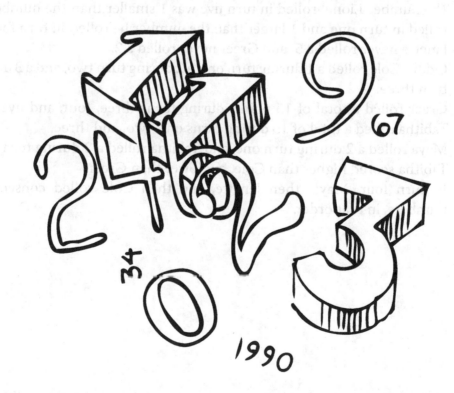

Take 5

A thunderstorm altered six friends' plans for a picnic. They decided to pass the time playing the dice game Take 5. Players get five rolls in order to try to obtain the highest score. Lionel won the first game by earning 20 points, the maximum possible. He rolled 6 + 5 + 4 + 3 + 2 = 20, so he did not roll a 1 during any turn. Eliminate 1 for Lionel on all five turns. Players rolled different numbers during their five turns. (Hint: This means that when you circle 4 for a player, you can cross out 4 in all of the other rounds, and so on.) Nobody rolled the same number as any other player during any turn. Check frequently for numbers that are the only ones in a column or row. Nobody got the same score as anyone else. Players scored 15, 16, 17, 18, 19, and 20 points. Write the scores in the bottom row when you know them. Determine the five numbers that each player rolled for each turn of Game 1. After marking them, use that information and the clues to find the results of Game 2.

Clues for Game 1:

1. Janette's score was higher than Maya's.
2. Lionel did not roll his 4 during turn two, four, or five.
3. Tabitha rolled a 6 during turn two.
4. Greer did not roll his 5 during turns one, four, or five.
5. The number Lionel rolled in turn five was 1 smaller than the number he rolled in turn one and 1 larger than the number he rolled in turn four.
6. Janette never rolled a 5, and Greer never rolled a 2.
7. Oddly, Cole rolled a 1 during turn one, a 2 during turn two, and a 3 during turn three.
8. Greer rolled a total of 15 points during turns three, four, and five, and Tabitha rolled a total of 15 during turns one, two, and three.
9. Maya rolled a 2 during turn one, and Tabitha rolled a 2 during turn five.
10. Tabitha scored higher than Cole, but lower than Greer.
11. In turn four, Maya, then Janette, and then Cole rolled consecutive numbers, in that order.

DOI: 10.4324/9781003236382-37

Use the clues for Game 1 to mark each player's roll of the die in five turns. You will need the results of Game 1 to learn the results of Game 2.

	Cole	Greer	Janette	Lionel	Maya	Tabitha
Turn One	1 2 3 4 5 6	1 2 3 4 5 6	1 2 3 4 5 6	1 2 3 4 5 6	1 2 3 4 5 6	1 2 3 4 5 6
Turn Two	1 2 3 4 5 6	1 2 3 4 5 6	1 2 3 4 5 6	1 2 3 4 5 6	1 2 3 4 5 6	1 2 3 4 5 6
Turn Three	1 2 3 4 5 6	1 2 3 4 5 6	1 2 3 4 5 6	1 2 3 4 5 6	1 2 3 4 5 6	1 2 3 4 5 6
Turn Four	1 2 3 4 5 6	1 2 3 4 5 6	1 2 3 4 5 6	1 2 3 4 5 6	1 2 3 4 5 6	1 2 3 4 5 6
Turn Five	1 2 3 4 5 6	1 2 3 4 5 6	1 2 3 4 5 6	1 2 3 4 5 6	1 2 3 4 5 6	1 2 3 4 5 6
Final Score				20		

Take 5, continued

Clues for Game 2:

1. Nobody rolled the same number during the same turn in Game 2 as they did in Game 1.
2. Cole never rolled a 4, and Maya never rolled a 1.
3. Tabitha's first three rolls totaled 6.
4. Greer rolled a 5 in turn four, and Cole rolled a 5 in turn five.
5. Cole was the only player who scored the same total in Game 1 as in Game 2.
6. Janette and Lionel both rolled 1, 4, and 5, in some order, during their first three turns.
7. In turn three, Cole rolled a lower number in Game 2 than in Game 1, while Greer's turn three roll was a higher number in Game 2 than in Game 1.
8. Lionel had a higher number in turns one and five of Game 2 than in turns one and five of Game 1.
9. Janette rolled a higher number in turn five than in turn one.
10. Tabitha rolled a lower number, by 2, in turn two than in turn three.
11. Cole's roll in turn one equaled the rolls he had in turns three and four.

Game 2

Use the clues for Game 2 to mark each player's roll of the die in five turns. Use the results of Game 1 to reveal the results of Game 2.

	Cole	Greer	Janette	Lionel	Maya	Tabitha
Turn One	1 2 3 4 5 6	1 2 3 4 5 6	1 2 3 4 5 6	1 2 3 4 5 6	1 2 3 4 5 6	1 2 3 4 5 6
Turn Two	1 2 3 4 5 6	1 2 3 4 5 6	1 2 3 4 5 6	1 2 3 4 5 6	1 2 3 4 5 6	1 2 3 4 5 6
Turn Three	1 2 3 4 5 6	1 2 3 4 5 6	1 2 3 4 5 6	1 2 3 4 5 6	1 2 3 4 5 6	1 2 3 4 5 6
Turn Four	1 2 3 4 5 6	1 2 3 4 5 6	1 2 3 4 5 6	1 2 3 4 5 6	1 2 3 4 5 6	1 2 3 4 5 6
Turn Five	1 2 3 4 5 6	1 2 3 4 5 6	1 2 3 4 5 6	1 2 3 4 5 6	1 2 3 4 5 6	1 2 3 4 5 6
Final Score						

Use these solutions to check students' work, or allow students to self-check.

To help teach logical thought, solutions are described step by step in the same order their clues appear. Please note that these solutions demonstrate the author's reasoning. You can use a different path of thinking and still get correct solutions. If you do not need help solving a given puzzle, you can skip to the end of the entry, where you will find a list of answers.

The introductions, charts, and clues included with each puzzle contain sufficient information to solve it. However, the logic required to solve some puzzles can be challenging. You may need more information to use a clue, so read the clues several times. If you are baffled, use the descriptions for help. Do not guess. Find information to verify your thinking.

Brackets indicate that relevant information was taken from an earlier clue. For example, [3] means that information from Clue 3 is being used. The use of parentheses or the notation "(only one)" indicates that this option is the only one remaining in a column or row, and you should circle it.

Who Will Be My Teacher? p. 9

Clue 1: For Thomsen, eliminate fifth grade for current grade and fourth grade for next year's grade.

Clue 2: Eliminate sixth and eighth grades for Nixon's current grade and second grade for Nixon's grade next year.

Clue 3: Clausing does not teach sixth grade and will not teach second grade next year, and second grade will not go with sixth grade. Use information later.

Clue 4: Nixon does not teach seventh grade now, and eliminate third and fourth grades for next year's grade. Then she teaches fifth grade now and will teach first grade next year (only ones).

Clue 5: Thomsen does not match up with second or seventh grades, so she teaches third grade (only one). Then Clausing will teach fourth grade, and Harris will teach second grade (only ones). Because Harris is the one who will teach second grade, she does not teach seventh grade now [5]. Then Clausing teaches seventh grade (only one).

Further Reasoning: Reviewing Clue 3, Harris will teach second grade next year [5], so she is not teaching sixth grade now. She is teaching eighth grade, and Thomsen teaches sixth grade (only ones).

Answers: Clausing, seventh grade, fourth grade; Harris, eighth grade, second grade; Nixon, fifth grade, first grade; Thomsen, sixth grade, third grade.

Face-Bond Friends   p. 10

Clue 1: Braxton matches up with 150 or 200 miles (mi), and 37 friends matches up with 75 or 100 mi. Braxton does not have 37 friends.

Clue 2: The only possibility is that the one with 34 friends matches up with 200 mi, Viola matches up with 100 mi (half of the one with 34 friends), and Kaela matches up with 75 mi (less than Viola). The girl with 34 friends is not Viola or Kaela.

Clue 3: Kaela and Viola did not drive 150 miles [2], so they do not have 29 friends.

Clue 4: Trexi does not have 46 or 34 friends (drove farther and less than those girls). Braxton has 34 friends (only one). Then Trexi has 29 friends (only one). Trexi drove 50 miles less than the person with 34 friends (Braxton), so Braxton drove 200 mi, and Trexi drove 150 mi. Trexi drove twice as far as the one with 46 friends, so the one with 46 friends drove 75 mi. Kaela drove 75 mi [2], so Kaela has 46 friends; Viola has 37 friends (only one).

Answers: Braxton, 34 friends, 200 mi; Kaela, 46 friends, 75 mi; Trexi, 29 friends, 150 mi; Viola, 37 friends, 100 mi.

Brr! Baby, It's Cold Outside   p. 11

Clue 1: The only decrease of 7 degrees for Odell is −1 on Sunday to −8 on Monday.

Clue 2: The only decrease of 7 degrees for Wendy is −4 on Tuesday to −11 on Wednesday.

Clue 3: The only increase of 9 degrees for Odell is −16 on Thursday to −7 on Friday.

Clue 4: The only increases of 1 degree for Harriet are −6 on Sunday to −5 on Monday, −15 on Tuesday to −14 on Wednesday, and −3 on Thursday to −2 on Friday. Then Odell reported −18 on Tuesday and −20 on Wednesday, and Wendy reported −10 on Sunday, −12 on Monday, −13 on Thursday, and −9 on Friday (only ones).

Answers: Harriet, −6, −5, −15, −14, −3, −2; Odell, −1, −8, −18, −20, −16, −7; Wendy, −10, −12, −4, −11, −13, −9.

Please Don't Take My Sunshine Away   p. 12

Calculations: Celsius: 27.22°, 29.44°, 31.67°; Fahrenheit: 78°, 83°, 86°, 93°.

Clue 1: Eliminate the two lowest temps (78° and 81°) for Terrence. Dharma's favorite wasn't the lowest (78°) or the highest (93°), and Bina's wasn't either of the two highest temps (89° or 93°).

Clue 2: Possibilities are that Adriel's favorite was 81°, 86°, or 89°; and Shinichi's was 78°, 83°, or 86°. Adriel's favorite was not 78°, 83°, 85°, or 93°. Shinichi's was not 81°, 85°, 89°, or 93°.

Clue 3: Neva's favorite wasn't either of the two lowest temps (78° or 81°). Bina's favorite wasn't the lowest (78°) or either of the highest two temps (89° or 93°) [1]. Ethan's favorite wasn't either of the two highest temps (89° or 93°), and it wasn't 86°, because his favorite was lower than Bina's.

Clue 4: Possibilities are that Terrence's favorite was 93°, 89°, or 85° (not 83° or 86°) and Neva's was 89° or 85° [3, not 81°]; Neva's favorite was not 93°, 86°, or 83°. Terrence's was 93° (only one), so Neva's was 89°.

Clue 5: Neva's favorite was 89° [4], so Adriel's was 30° C.

Clue 6: Shinichi's temperature was not the lowest, 25.56° (78°; warmer than Bina's). Ethan's favorite was the lowest temp of 25.56° (78°; only one). Shinichi's favorite was 28.33° (only one), so Bina's was 27.22°. Dharma's was 85° (29.44°; only one).

Answers: Ethan, 25.56° (78°); Bina, 27.22° (81°); Shinichi, 28.33° (83°); Dharma, 29.44° (85°); Adriel, 30° (86°); Neva, 31.67° (89°); Terrence, 33.89° (93°).

Century Club   p. 14

Clue 1: Talon does not have 30 wheels. Infinity does not have 30 wheels.

Clue 2: Infiniti does not have 20 mirrors.

Clue 3: Hummer does not have 10 or 30 handles. Viper does not have 30 or 40 handles.

Clue 4: Infiniti does not have 10 handles. Talon does not have 40 handles.

Clue 5: Hummer does not have 40 handles. Then Hummer has 20 handles (only one). Nobody else has 20 handles. Then Viper has 10 handles, Infiniti has 40, and Talon has 30 (only ones). Hummer doesn't have 20 or 40 wheels, 20 lights, or 20 mirrors. Infiniti does not have 40 wheels, 40 lights, or 40 mirrors. Talon does not have 30 lights, 30 wheels, or 30 mirrors. Viper does not have 10 wheels, 10 lights, or 10 mirrors.

Clue 6: Infiniti does not have 30 lights.

Clue 7: Infiniti does not have 10 wheels; she has 20 wheels (only one), so Talon has 10 wheels. Then Hummer has 30 wheels, and Viper has 40 wheels (only ones). Hummer does not have 30 lights or 30 mirrors. Infiniti does not have 20 lights. Talon does not have 10 lights or 10 mirrors. Viper does not have 40 lights or 40 mirrors. Then Infiniti has 10 lights, Hummer has 40, Talon has 20, and Viper has 30 (only ones). Then Hummer does not have 40 mirrors, Infiniti does not have 10 mirrors, Talon does not have 20 mirrors, and Viper does not have 30 mirrors. Hummer has 10 mirrors, Infiniti has 30, Talon has 40, and Viper has 20 (only ones).

Answers: Hummer, 20 handles, 40 lights, 10 mirrors, 30 wheels; Infiniti, 40 handles, 10 lights, 30 mirrors, 20 wheels; Talon, 30 handles, 20 lights, 40 mirrors, 10 wheels; Viper, 10 handles, 30 lights, 20 mirrors, 40 wheels.

I'm Done! What Should I Do Now? p. 15

Clue 1: Strategy game matches up with 156 points.

Clue 2: Eadin and Cass were partners. They did not get 156 points [1, strategy game].

Clue 3: Claudette did a math puzzler, so she did not get 156 points [1, strategy] or 204 points.

Clue 4: Hayley did not work with Noah. They did not play a strategy game or get 156 points. Use information later.

Clue 5: Karen did not work with Claudette or Margaret.

Clue 6: Only possibility is 52 points for Eadin and Cass [2, card players] and 156 for Margaret and her partner. Noah did not work with Margaret.

Clue 7: Noah did a math puzzler, so he was with Claudette [3]. Cass got 52 points [6], so Claudette and Noah got 104 points.

Clue 8: The only possibility for Ronald is 156 points, so he was with Margaret [6]. Dave was Sharon's partner. They scored 26 points. Karen was with Hayley (only one). They got 204 points (only one).

Answers: Claudette, Noah, 104 points; Eadin, Cass, 52 points; Hayley, Karen, 204 points; Margaret, Ronald, 156 points; Sharon, Dave, 26 points.

24 Game® p. 16

Calculations: These are some possible solutions, although there may be others.
Game 1: $1 - 5 - 7 - 8$ is $(7 + 1) \times (8 - 5)$; $4 - 5 - 7 - 8$ is $(8 + 4) \times (7 - 5)$ or $(5 + 8 + 7 + 4)$; $1 - 6 - 8 - 9$ is $(1 + 9 + 6 + 8)$ or $(9 - 6) \times (8 \div 1)$; $1 - 6 - 8 - 8$ is $[(8 + 1) - 6] \times 8$. Game 2: $1 - 2 - 2 - 7$ is $(2 + 2) \times (7 - 1)$; $1 - 2 - 6 - 7$ is $(1 + 7) \times (6 \div 2)$; $1 - 1 - 2 - 9$ is $(9 - 1) \times (2 + 1)$; $1 - 2 - 5 - 6$ is $(1 + 5) \times (6 - 2)$.

Clue 1: Jerry and Paul could have been the ones with 1, 2, and 6 $(1 - 2 - 6 - 7$ and $1 - 2 - 5 - 6)$ or 1, 2, and 7 $(1 - 2 - 2 - 7$ and $1 - 2 - 6 - 7)$. They could not have had $1 - 1 - 2 - 9$ (no others have 1, 2, and 9).

Clue 2: Common numbers are 5, 7, and 8 $(1 - 5 - 7 - 8$ and $4 - 5 - 7 - 8)$ or 1, 6, and 8 $(1 - 6 - 8 - 9$ and $1 - 6 - 8 - 8)$. Because Tamara and Collene did not have $1 - 5 - 7 - 8$, they also did not have $4 - 5 - 7 - 8$. They had $1 - 6 - 8 - 9$ and $1 - 6 - 8 - 8$, so Jerry and Paul cannot have had $1 - 6 - 8 - 9$ and $1 - 6 - 8 - 8$.

Clue 3: Only $1 + 2 + 2 + 7 = 12$, so those were Collene's Game 2 numbers. Then $1 - 1 - 2 - 9$ were Tamara's (only one).

Clue 4: The only numbers in Game 1 that add up to 24 are 4 – 5 – 7 – 8 and 1 – 6 – 8 – 9. Paul did not get 1 – 6 – 8 – 9 [2], so his numbers were 4 – 5 – 7 – 8. Then Jerry got 1 – 5 – 7 – 8 (only one).

Clue 5: Collene used 1 – 2 – 2 – 7 (not 1 – 2 – 5 – 6) in Game 2 [3], so Paul must have used 1 – 2 – 5 – 6; then Jerry got 1 – 2 – 6 – 7 (only one).

Clue 6: Tamara and Jerry did not add to get 8 x 3 in Game 1, so Collene and Paul added [3]. Collene has 1 + 6 + 8 + 9. Then Tamara has 1 – 6 – 8 – 8 (only one).

Answers: Collene, 1 – 6 – 8 – 9 and 1 – 2 – 2 – 7; Jerry, 1 – 5 – 7 – 8 and 1 – 2 – 6 – 7; Paul, 4 – 5 – 7 – 8 and 1 – 2 – 5 – 6; Tamara, 1 – 6 – 8 – 8 and 1 – 1 – 2 – 9.

Cha-Ching
p. 18

Calculations: Nickels: $2.25, $2.40, $3.00, $3.45; dimes: $2.00, $3.80, $4.00, $4.60; quarters: $5.75, $6.50, $7.00, $8.25.

Clue 1: Lancaster did not save 45 or 48 nickels, Quinton did not save 45 or 69 nickels, and Nigel did not save 60 or 69 nickels.

Clue 2: Nigel did not save 23 or 26 quarters, Quinton did not save 23 or 33 quarters, and Lancaster did not save 28 or 33 quarters.

Clue 3: Nigel had 48 or 45 nickels [1]. The only number 10 fewer than one of those is 38, so Nigel had 48 nickels ($2.40), and Lancaster had 38 dimes ($3.80). Then Quinton had 60 nickels (only one; $3.00). Lancaster had 69 nickels (only one; $3.45). Then Treyton had 45 nickels (only one; $2.25).

Clue 4: Treyton had $2.25 in nickels [3], so he had $2.00 in dimes (20 dimes). Treyton must have had $8.25 in quarters (33 quarters) to have $6.00 more than his nickels' total of $2.25. Then Nigel had 28 quarters (only one; $7.00). Quinton had 26 quarters (only one; $6.50). Lancaster had 23 quarters (only one; $5.75).

Clue 5: Treyton's total was $12.50, so Quinton had $13.50. Quinton's nickels totaled $3.00, and his quarters total $6.50 (total of $9.50), so his dimes must have totaled $4.00 (40 dimes). Nigel must have had 46 dimes (only one; $4.60).

Answers: Lancasater, 69 nickels, 38 dimes, 23 quarters ($13.00); Nigel, 48 nickels, 46 dimes, 28 quarters ($14.00); Quinton, 60 nickels, 40 dimes, 26 quarters ($13.50); Treyton, 45 nickels, 20 dimes, 33 quarters ($12.50). Nigel had the highest total.

Rah, Rah! Go, Team!
p. 20

Clue 1: Meyer and Upton do not root for the Cyclones or the Sailors, and their teams do not wear blue/green/red or green/blue. Beane, Lance, and Paulson's teams did not score 68 points. The Bears did not score 68 points. Beane, Lance, and Paulson do not root for the Bears.

Clue 2: Beane's and Lance's teams' colors are not blue/red/white or red/white. Meyer, Paulson, and Upton's teams did not have 76 points.

Clue 3: The Bears did not score 68 [1], 74, or 76 points. The Sailors did not score 68, 70 (Bears did not score 68), or 76 points, and the Cyclones did not score 68, 70, or 72. Use information later.

Clue 4: The Paulson team did not score 68 [1], 74, or 76. Lance's team did not score 68, 70, or 76. Beane's team scored 76 (only one). Then Lance's team scored 74, and Paulson's scored 72.

Clue 5: Use information later.

Clue 6: Meyer's team does not wear blue/red/white or red/white; they wear green/white (only one).

Clue 7: Beane's team scored 76 points [4], so Beane's team is the Panthers. Lance's team scored 74 points [4], and the Cyclones scored 74 points [3], so Lance roots for the Cyclones [3]. Paulson's team scored 72 points [4], and the Sailors scored 72 points [3], so Paulson roots for the Sailors [3, only one]. The Bears scored 70 points. Use information later.

Clue 8: The Bears is not the Uptons' team. The Bears is the Meyers' team (only one), and the Upton family roots for the Jaguars. The Bears did not score 68 [1, 8], so the Meyers family's team did not score 68. The Meyers' team scored 70, and the Upton family's team scored 68. The Upton family's team wears red/white. The Paulson family's team wears blue/red/white (only one).

Further Reasoning: Reviewing Clue 5, the Cyclones do not wear any red or white. The Lance family's team [7, Cyclones] doesn't wear blue/green/red, so it wears green/blue. Then the Beane family's team wears blue/green/red (only one).

Answers: Beane, Panthers, blue/green/red, 76 points; Lance, Cyclones, green/blue, 74 points; Meyer, Bears, green/white, 70 points; Paulson, Sailors, blue/red/white, 72 points; Upton, Jaguars, red/white, 68 points.

NBA Salaries Are Not Dribble   p. 22

Clue 1: The only difference that works out exactly is that S. O'Neal got $21,000,000 ('08–'09) and Garnett got $18,832,044 ('10–'11). Cross out $21,000,000 for S. O'Neal ('09–'10 and '10–'11). Cross out $18,832,044 for Garnett ('08–'09 and '09–'10) and $24,751,000 for Garnett ('10–'11), because players can't have two incomes in one season.

Clue 2: Lewis made $19,573,511 ('10–'11), and Duncan made $22,183,218 ('09–'10). Cross out $19,573,511 for Lewis ('08–'09 and '09–'10), $22,183,218 for Duncan ('08–'09 and '10–'11), and $18,835,381 for Duncan ('09–'10).

Clue 3: Garnett made $24,751,000 ('08–'09), and J. O'Neal made $21,372,000 ('08–'09). Cross out $22,995,000 ('08–'09) and $21,372,000 ('09–'10 and '10–'11) for J. O'Neal. Cross out $24,751,000 ('09–'10) for Garnett.

Clue 4: Bryant made $23,034,375 ('09–'10), and Duncan made $18,835,381 ('10–'11). Cross out $21,262,500 and $24,806,250 ('09–'10) and $23,034,375 ('08–'09 and '10–'11) for Bryant. Cross out $18,835,381 ('08–'09) for Duncan. Then Duncan made $18,835,381 for '10–'11 (only one).

Clue 5: McGrady made $23,329,561 ('09–'10), and Bryant made $21,262,500 ('08–'09). Cross out $23,329,561 ('08–'09 and '10–'11) for McGrady. Cross out $21,262,500 ('10–'11) and $24,806,250 ('08–'09) for Bryant. Then Bryant made $24,806,250 ('10–'11; only one).

Further Reasoning: Four players' salaries are listed for each season [Intro]. Four players are already circled for 2008–2009 (S. O'Neal, Bryant, J. O'Neal, and Garnett). Four are circled for 2010–2011 (Garnett, Duncan, Lewis, and Bryant), so J. O'Neal must be the fourth player for 2009–2010 ($22,995,000). Cross out $22,995,000 for J. O'Neal ('10–'11).

Answers: For 2008–2009, Shaquille O'Neal made $21,000,000; Kobe Bryant made $21,262,500; Jermaine O'Neal made $21,372,000; and Kevin Garnett made $24,751,000. For 2009–2010, Tim Duncan made $22,183,218; Jermaine O'Neal made $22,995,000; Kobe Bryant made $23,034,375; and Tracy McGrady made $23,329,561. For 2010–2011, Kevin Garnett made $18,832,044; Tim Duncan made $18,835,381; Rashard Lewis made $19,573,511; and Kobe Bryant made $24,806,250.

Triple Trials   p. 24

Calculations: .0625 in. = 1.5875 mm; .125 in. = 3.175 mm; .25 in = 6.35 mm; .375 in. = .9525 cm; .5 in. = 1.27 cm; .625 in. = 1.5875 cm; 36 in. = .914 m; 45 in. = 1.143 m; 48 in. = 1.219 m.

Clue 1: The cell phone button was .25 in. (6.35 mm). Use information later.

Clue 2: The refrigerator was 36 in. (.914 m). This girl did not have a calculator. Use information later.

Clue 3: Brooke measured .125 in. (3.175 mm).

Clue 4: Natalie's seam was a standard ⅝-in. (.625 in.) wide. That is 1.5875 cm.

Clue 5: One girl matches up with ⅜ in. (.375 in.) and 48 in. (1.219 m). Use information later.

Clue 6: Emma (10) is the middle sister [Intro], so she measured .5 in. (1.27 cm). Then Brooke measured the ⅜-in. (.375-in.) screw (only one) and the 48-in. (1.219-m) drywall [5].

Clue 7: Natalie measured the .0625 in. (1.5875 mm) lid. Then Emma measured .25 in. (6.35 mm; only one).

Further Reasoning: Reviewing Clue 2, the 36-in. (.9144 m) guess was not made by Natalie, who had a calculator [7]; it was made by Emma (only one). Then Natalie measured 45 in. (1.145 m).

Answers: Brooke, .125 in. = 3.175 mm, .375 in. = .9525 cm, 48 in. = 1.219 m; Emma, .25 in = 6.35 mm, .5 in. = 1.27 cm, 36 in. = .9144 m; Natalie, .0625 in. = .15875 mm, .625 in. = 1.5875 cm, 45 in. = 1.143 m.

How Big and How Far? p. 26

Clue 1: Ames and Fort Dodge could be 214.3 mi and 217.4 mi or 256.99 mi and 257.25 mi away from Minneapolis. Use information later.

Clue 2: Ames is 34.3 mi from Des Moines. Waukee is 17.1 mi from Des Moines.

Clue 3: 4,097 x 4.5 = 18,437, which is not a choice. 12,641 x 4.5 = 56,884. 25,075 x 4.5 = 112,837, which is too large. Waukee has a population of 12,641, and Ames has a population of slightly fewer than 56,884, which means it has 56,814.

Clue 4: Jefferson is either 73.5 mi or 95 mi from Des Moines. 73.5 x 3.5 = 257.25, so the distance from Jefferson to Des Moines is 73.5 mi, and the distance from Jefferson to Minneapolis is 257.25 mi. Then the distance from Fort Dodge to Des Moines is 95 mi (only one).

Clue 5: Ames's population is 56,814 [3], and half of that is 28,407; the number nearest to this is 25,075 for Fort Dodge. Waukee's population is 12,641 [3], and a third of that is 4214; the nearest to that number is 4,097 for Jefferson.

Clue 6: The distance from Jefferson to Minneapolis is 257.5 mi [4], and 257.5 − 40 = 217.5, so Fort Dodge is 217.4 mi from Minneapolis.

Further Reasoning: Reviewing Clue 1, Fort Dodge is 217.4 mi from Minneapolis, so Ames is 214.3 mi to Minneapolis. Then Waukee is 256.99 mi from Minneapolis (only one).

Answers: Ames, 56,814 people, 34.3 mi to Des Moines, 214.3 mi to Minneapolis; Fort Dodge, 25,075 people, 95 mi to Des Moines, 217.4 mi to Minneapolis; Jefferson, 4,097 people, 73.5 mi to Des Moines, 257.5 mi to Minneapolis; Waukee, 12,641 people, 17.1 mi to Des Moines, 256.99 mi to Minneapolis.

Saturated Saturday p. 27

Calculations: Swimming: ¾ hr, 1 hr, ½ hr, ¾ hr. Ball game: 1 ¾ hr, 1 ¼ hr, 2 ½ hr, 2 ¼ hr. Picnic: 3 hr, 3 ½ hr, 2 ¼ hr, 1 ¾ hr.

Clue 1: The 8:45–9:45 swim matches up with the 3:30–7:00 picnic. Use information later.

Clue 2: The 12:45–2:00 game matches up with either the 8:00–8:45 or the 10:15–11:00 swim lesson. Use information later.

Clue 3: Floyd's swim time was not at 8:00, and Horace's swim time was not at 10:15. Horace's game was not at 12:30, and Floyd's game was not at 1:30.

Clue 4: Jinjer's game was not 1:15–3:45 (2 ½ hr), and Horace's was not 12:45–2:00 (1 ¼ hr). Horace's game was not at 12:30 [3] or 12:45 [4] and it was not the latest (Jinjer's was later), so it started at 1:15, and Jinjer's started later, at 1:30.

Clue 5: Jinjer's picnic was not 5:00–6:45 (1 ¾ hr), and Horace's picnic was not 3:30–7:00 (3 ½ hr).

Clue 6: Horace's swim time was not 9:30–10:00 (½ hr), and Jinjer's swim was not 8:45–9:45 (1 hr). Floyd's swim time was not 9:30–10:00 (½ hr), and Dixie's swim time was not 8:45–9:45 (1 hr).

Further Reasoning: Reviewing Clue 1, Jinjer and Dixie did not have 1-hr swim lessons (8:45–9:45), so they did not attend 3 ½-hour picnics. Floyd did (only one), so Floyd had a 1-hr swim lesson. Horace had a swim lesson from 8:00–8:45 (45 min; only one). Jinjer's swim lesson was shorter than Horace's [6], so she had a 30-min lesson (9:30–10:00). Dixie had a swim lesson from 10:15–11:00. Reviewing Clue 2, the 12:45 game matches up with Dixie or Floyd. Dixie's lesson was 45 min, so Dixie's game was at 12:45, and Floyd's was at 12:30 (only one). Each stayed the full time at each activity [Intro], so Horace and Jinjer didn't have a 3:00 picnic (their games lasted until 3:45). Jinjer had a 4:30 picnic (2 ¼ hr; only one). Horace had a 5:00–6:45 picnic, and Dixie had a 3:00–6:00 picnic (only ones).

Answers: Dixie, 10:15 swim, 12:45 game, 3:00 picnic; Floyd, 8:45 swim, 12:30 game, 3:30 picnic; Horace, 8:00 swim, 1:15 game, 5:00 picnic; Jinjer, 9:30 swim, 1:30 game, 4:30 picnic.

Movies and Music Are Marvelous p. 28

Clue 1: Craig was not born in 1992 or 1988 (older than at least two others). Dale and Elizabeth were not born in 1978 (aren't the oldest). Franz was not born in 1978 or 1980 (younger than at least two others). Georgia and Bethenny were not born in 1992 (youngest).

Clue 2: Georgia has 42, 62, or 78 movies and 126, 186, or 234 CDs. The only possibility is that somebody has 82 movies and 164 CDs, and that person is Bethenny or Elizabeth [Intro, girls].

Clue 3: The only possibilities are that Craig was born in 1978 (Bethenny was not born in 1992 [1]), Bethenny was born in 1988, Dale was born in 1982, and Franz was born in 1992.

Clue 4: Craig has 42, 62, or 78 movies and 126, 186, or 234 CDs. Craig does not have 234 CDs (fewer than Georgia), so he does not have 78 movies. Georgia does not have 126 (Craig's lowest possibility; she has more than that), so she does not have 42 movies [2]. Dale does not have 234 or 186 CDs (fewer than Craig and Georgia).

Clue 5: Bethenny and Craig have 82, 62, or 56 movies; Dale and Franz have 62, 42, or 36 movies. Craig does not have 82 or 56 movies [4], so he has 62 movies, and Franz has 42. Dale has 36 (only one), so Bethenny has 56. Then Georgia has 78 movies, and Elizabeth has 82 (only ones). Then Craig has 186 CDs [4], and Georgia has 234 CDs [2].

Clue 6: Franz is the youngest [3, 1992], so he does not have 78 CDs.

Clue 7: Dale, who was born in 1982 [3], does not have 82 CDs. Elizabeth has 82 movies [5], so she was born in 1980. Georgia was born in 1986 (only one).

Clue 8: Dale does not have 78 CDs (least), so has 126 CDs. Then Franz has 82 CDs, and Bethenny has 78 CDs. Elizabeth has 164 CDs [2, twice her number of movies].

Answers: Bethenny, 1988, 56 movies, 78 CDs; Craig, 1978, 62 movies, 186 CDs; Dale, 1982, 36 movies, 126 CDs; Elizabeth, 1980, 82 movies, 164 CDs; Franz, 1992, 42 movies, 82 CDs; Georgia, 1986, 78 movies; 234 CDs.

We're Crazy Over Algebra   p. 30

Calculations: $2n + 7 = 3n - 1$ ($n = 8$); $4n - 5 = 3n - 2$ ($n = 3$); $5n - 9 = 3n + 3$ ($n = 6$); $4n + 6 = 6n - 4$ ($n = 5$); $3n + 5 = 2n + 6$ ($n = 1$).

Clue 1: Jillian and Hakeem were partners. They did not solve $n = 8$ or $n = 3$.

Clue 2: Ellen and Tawny [Intro, girls] were not with Lia. Ellen, Jillian, and Tawny did not solve $5n - 9 = 3n + 3$ ($n = 6$).

Clue 3: Frank did not solve $n = 3$.

Clue 4: Ellen did not solve $n = 8$ (eight), Frank did not solve $n = 5$ (five), and Tawny did not solve $n = 3$ (three).

Clue 5: Frank [3] and Winston [Intro, boy] did not solve $n = 5$.

Clue 6: These five do not go together. You can see that the second, fourth, and fifth people described are girls, so the first and third must be boys. This means that $n = 8$ was solved by Winston (could not have been solved by Frank or any of the girls). The five different people are Frank, the girl who worked with Fiona (this must be Ellen, because Tawny is another person mentioned in the clue), the one who solved $n = 8$, Tawny, and the one who solved $3n + 5 = 2n + 6$ ($n = 1$) with Hakeem. Frank did not solve $n = 8$ or $n = 1$ (other people mentioned in the clue found these), so he solved $n = 6$ (only one), and he did not work with Fiona. The girl who worked with Fiona is Ellen, because she isn't

Tawny or the one who got n = 1 with Hakeem. Ellen solved n = 3 (only one). Tawny solved n = 5, not n = 1 with Hakeem. Jillian worked with Hakeem, so they solved n = 1.

Further Reasoning: Reviewing Clue 2, Lia helped get n = 6, and Frank solved n = 6, so Lia was with Frank. Reviewing Clue 5, Tawny solved 4n + 6 = 6n − 4 (n = 5), so she was not with Seeley. She was with Bradford, and Winston was with Seeley (only ones).

Answers: Ellen and Fiona, 4n − 5 = 3n − 2 (n = 3); Frank and Lia, 5n − 9 = 3n + 3 (n = 6); Jillian and Hakeem, 3n + 5 = 2n + 6 (n = 1). Tawny and Bradford, 4n + 6 = 6n − 4 (n = 5); Winston and Seeley, 2n + 7 = 3n − 1 (n = 8).

Spice It Up   p. 31

Calculations: Pepper: 1 tsp = $\frac{1}{6}$ oz, 1 $\frac{1}{2}$ tsp = $\frac{1}{4}$ oz, 2 tsp = $\frac{1}{3}$ oz, 2 $\frac{1}{2}$ tsp = $\frac{5}{12}$ oz; chives: $\frac{1}{4}$ Tbsp = $\frac{1}{8}$ oz, $\frac{1}{3}$ Tbsp = $\frac{1}{6}$ oz, $\frac{1}{2}$ Tbsp = $\frac{1}{4}$ oz, $\frac{2}{3}$ Tbsp = $\frac{1}{3}$ oz; mustard: $\frac{1}{16}$ c = $\frac{1}{2}$ oz, $\frac{1}{8}$ c = 1 oz, $\frac{3}{16}$ c = 1 $\frac{1}{2}$ oz, $\frac{1}{4}$ c = 2 oz.

Clue 1: The possibilities for Rosemary's mustard are 1, 1 $\frac{1}{2}$, and 2 oz; the possibilities for Myrtle's pepper are $\frac{1}{6}$, $\frac{1}{4}$, and $\frac{1}{3}$ oz. A sixth of Rosemary's $\frac{1}{2}$ oz is $\frac{1}{12}$ oz (no amount for Myrtle), and six times Myrtle's $\frac{5}{12}$ oz is 2 $\frac{1}{2}$ oz (no amount for Rosemary).

Clue 2: The possibilities are 1, 1 $\frac{1}{2}$, and 2 oz for Rosemary's mustard and $\frac{1}{6}$, $\frac{1}{4}$, and $\frac{1}{3}$ oz for Ginger's chives. A sixth of Rosemary's $\frac{1}{2}$ oz is $\frac{1}{12}$ oz (no amount for Ginger); and six times Ginger's $\frac{1}{8}$ oz is $\frac{3}{4}$ oz (no amount for Rosemary).

Clue 3: Basil does not use $\frac{5}{12}$ oz pepper (not an amount for Myrtle's chives).

Clue 4: The possibilities are 1, 1 $\frac{1}{2}$, and 2 oz for Ginger's mustard and $\frac{1}{6}$, $\frac{1}{4}$, and $\frac{1}{3}$ oz for Basil's chives. A sixth of Ginger's $\frac{1}{2}$ oz is $\frac{1}{12}$ oz (no amount for Basil); and six times Basil's $\frac{1}{8}$ oz is $\frac{3}{4}$ oz (no amount for Ginger).

Clue 5: The possibilities are 1, 1 $\frac{1}{2}$, and 2 oz for Ginger's mustard and $\frac{1}{6}$, $\frac{1}{4}$, and $\frac{1}{3}$ oz for Rosemary's pepper. A sixth of Ginger's $\frac{1}{2}$ oz is $\frac{1}{12}$ oz (no amount for Rosemary), and six times Rosemary's $\frac{5}{12}$ oz is 2 $\frac{1}{2}$ oz (no amount for Ginger). Ginger is $\frac{5}{12}$ oz pepper (only one).

Clue 6: The only $\frac{1}{8}$-oz difference is if Ginger uses $\frac{1}{4}$ oz. chives and Rosemary uses $\frac{1}{8}$ oz. chives.

Clue 7: Basil's mustard amount is not $\frac{1}{2}$ oz (least) or 1 oz (Rosemary's smallest), and Rosemary's is not 2 oz (most). Myrtle's is $\frac{1}{2}$ oz (only one).

Further Reasoning: Reviewing Clue 1, Rosemary uses 1 or 1 $\frac{1}{2}$ oz mustard, so Myrtle uses $\frac{1}{6}$ or $\frac{1}{4}$ oz pepper (not $\frac{1}{3}$ oz). Reviewing Clue 2, Ginger uses $\frac{1}{4}$ oz chives [6], so Rosemary uses 1 $\frac{1}{2}$ oz mustard. Then Basil uses 2 oz mustard [7], and Ginger uses 1 oz mustard (only one). Because Rosemary uses 1 $\frac{1}{2}$ oz mustard, Myrtle uses $\frac{1}{4}$ oz. pepper [1]. Reviewing Clue 4, Ginger uses

1 oz mustard, so Basil uses ⅙ oz chives. Then Myrtle uses ⅓ oz chives (only one). Reviewing Clue 3, Myrtle uses ⅓ oz chives, so Basil uses ⅓ oz pepper. Then Rosemary uses ⅙ oz pepper (only one) [5].

Answers: Basil, ⅓ oz pepper, ⅙ oz chives, 2 oz mustard; Ginger, ⁵⁄₁₂ oz pepper, ¼ oz chives, 1 oz mustard; Myrtle; ¼ oz pepper, ⅓ oz chives, ½ oz mustard; Rosemary, ⅙ oz pepper, ⅛ oz chives, 1 ½ oz mustard.

Got Feet? p. 32

Calculations:

	Inches	Feet	Yards	Rods
Board	15	1 ¼	⁵⁄₁₂	³⁄₄₀
	27	2 ¼	¾	¹⁷⁄₁₂₅
	54	4 ½	1 ½	³⁄₁₁
	72	6	2	⁴⁄₁₁
String	30	2 ½	⅚	⁵⁄₃₃
	60	5	1 ⅔	¹⁰⁄₃₃
	99	8 ¼	2 ¾	½
	132	11	3 ⅔	⅔
Hose	72	6	2	⁴⁄₁₁
	126	10 ½	3 ½	⁷⁄₁₁
	180	15	5	¹⁰⁄₁₁
	297	24 ¾	8 ¼	1 ½
Rope	396	33	11	2
	528	44	14 ⅔	2 ⅔
	990	82 ½	27 ½	5
	1,254	104 ½	34 ⅚	6 ⅓

Clue 1: Dex and Millard did not have the 72-in. board or the 2-yd (72-in.) hose [Intro, boys].

Clue 2: Hester and Keysha did not have the 11-ft string or the 8 ¼-yd hose [Intro, girls].

Clue 3: Keysha had either a 27-in. board or a 2 ½-ft string, and Hester had either a 54-in. board or a 5-ft string. Use information later.

Clue 4: Hester had either a 54-in. board or a 5-ft string, and Millard had either a 27-in. board or a 2 ½-ft string. Use information later.

Further Reasoning: Together, Clues 2 and 3 show that Hester had both of the larger quantities, so she had the 54-in. board and the 5-ft string. Keysha had the 72-in. board (only one). She also had the 72-in. (2 yd) hose [1]. Because Keysha did not have the 27-in. board, Millard had the 27-in. board [4], and Keysha had the 2 ½-ft string [3]. Dex had the 15-in. board (only one).

Clue 5: Dex had the 15-in. board [4], so he had 3 ½-yd hose. Hester had the 5-yd hose, and Millard had the 8 ¼-yd hose (only ones). Clue 2 said that a boy had the longest hose and string, so Millard's string was 11 ft long (had longest hose). Dex's string was 8 ¼ ft long (only one).

Clue 6: Millard's string was 11 ft long (⅔ rd), so Keysha's rope was 2 ⅔ rd long (44 ft).

Clue 7: Millard's rope was 2 rd long, and Dex's rope was 5 rd long. Hester's rope was 6 ⅓ rd (only one).

Answers: Dex, 15 in. (board), 8 ½ ft (string), 3 ½ yd (hose), 5 rd (rope); Hester, 54 in. (board), 5 ft (string), 5 yd (hose), 6 ⅓ rd (rope); Keysha, 72 in. (board), 2 ½ ft (string), 2 yd (hose), 2 ⅔ rd (rope); Millard, 27 in. (board), 11 ft (string), 8 ¼ yd (hose), 2 rd (rope).

Boys Love Big Toys   p. 34

Calculations: A full ship is 128,000,000 lb; a full rail car is 200,000 lb; and a full semi is 54,000 lb.

Clue 1: The 47,250-lb semi (⅞ full) matches up with the 80,000,000-lb ship. Use information later.

Clue 2: Marquette did not have the 96,000,000-lb ship, the 150,000-lb rail car, or the 40,500-lb semi. Duluth will have two vehicles ¾ full. Use information later.

Clue 3: The 125,000-lb rail car matches up with the 102,400,000-lb ship. Use information later.

Clue 4: The only possibility is the 160,000-lb rail car for Marquette and the 80,000,000-lb ship for Beaumont. In Clue 1, the 80,000,000-lb ship is with the 47,250-lb semi, so Beaumont is also with the 47,250-lb semi (⅞ full). In Clue 3, the 125,000-lb rail car is with the 102,400,000-lb ship (⅘ full). Marquette did not have the 125,000-lb rail car, so he did not have the 102,400,000-lb ship; he had the 112,000,000-lb ship (only one). Beaumont did not have the 102,400,000-lb ship (⅘ full), so he did not have the 125,000-lb rail car (⅝ full).

Clue 5: Trenton's ship was 102,400,000 lb (⅘ full); Duluth's ship was 96,000,000 lb. Then Trenton also had the 125,000-lb rail car with the ⅘-full ship [3]. Trenton did not have the 33,750-lb semi, and Duluth did not have the 43,200-lb semi.

Clue 6: Beaumont's was not heaviest rail car, so his did not weigh 175,000 lb. Duluth's weighed this much (only one). Beaumont tracked the 150,000-lb. rail car (only one).

Further Reasoning: Reviewing Clue 2, Duluth's ship was ¾ full, and his rail car was not ¾ full (Beaumont's was), so his semi must have been ¾ full; it weighed 40,500 lb. Marquette's semi weighed 33,750 lb, and Trenton's semi weighed 43,200 lb (only ones).

Answers: Beaumont, 80,000,000 lb (ship), 150,000 lb (rail car), 47,250 lb (semi); Duluth, 96,000,000 lb (ship), 175,000 lb (rail car), 40,500 lb (semi); Marquette, 112,000,000 lb (ship), 160,000 lb (rail car), 33,750 lb (semi); Trenton, 102,400,000 lb (ship), 125,000 lb (rail car), 43,200 lb (semi).

Pigskin Playoffs   p. 36

Clue 1: Calculate four touchdowns (24 points) + four extra points (4 points) + one field goal (3 points) = 31 points for Discher in Game 2. (This is the answer to the example question.)

Clue 2: Use information later.

Clue 3: In both Game 1 and Game 3, 49 points were scored. Looking at the possible scores, Game 1 must have had a score of 21 (loser; three touchdowns + three extra points) to 28 (winner; four touchdowns + four extra points) for a total of 49 points (seven touchdowns + seven extra points). (Write "1" in the left column next to the lines for 21 and 28.) In Game 2, the losing team had 30 points [1, Discher won with 31 points]. Game 3's only possible score is 14 (two touchdowns + two extra points) to 35 (five touchdowns + five extra points) for a total of 49 (seven touchdowns + seven extra points). Then 27 and 42 are the scores for Game 4.

Clue 4: Game 5 was won with 20 points (three touchdowns + two extra points). Game 6 was won with 24 points (three touchdowns + three extra points + one field goal).

Clue 5: The only possible combination is 21 points on Friday and 42 points on Saturday. Looking at Clue 2, Linden played Game 4 (even) on Saturday, so Linden played odd games, 1 and 5, with Clayborn on Friday and Sunday. So Clayborn scored 28 points in Game 1 to beat Linden, who scored 21 points. Kremer scored 30 points in Game 2 (only one). Linden did not win Sunday's game, so they did not score 20 or 24 [4, winning scores]. Because Linden and Clayborn played Games 1 and 5 (odd), Clayborn played Linden on Sunday in Game 5 and won with 20 points [4].

Clue 6: This Game 6 score was 16 points (two touchdowns + two extra points + one two-point conversion). Then Linden scored 17 points in Game 5 [2, odd game].

Clue 7: Kremer won Game 6, so they scored 24 points [4]. Then Discher scored 16 (only one).

Clue 8: Clayborn scored 28 points on Friday, so they scored 14 points on Saturday.

Clue 9: Discher's Friday score was 31, so their Saturday score was 35. Kremer scored 27 points on Saturday (only one).

Answers: Clayborn, 28, 14, 20; Discher, 31, 35, 16; Kremer, 30, 27, 24; Linden, 21, 42, 17. Game 1's score was 28–21; Game 2's score was 31–30; Game 3's score was 35–14; Game 4's score was 42–27; Game 5's score was 20–17; Game 6's score was 24–16.

What's My G.P.A.? p. 38

Clue 1: Pearce had a 3.4 or a 3.75 average in math (not 3.9, 3.55, or 3.2). Victor had a 3.2 or a 3.55 average in math (not 3.9, 3.75, or 3.4).

Clue 2: The only possible combination is a 3.87 average in reading and a 3.825 in science. It is a girl, so Pearce and Victor [Intro, boys] did not get a 3.87 in reading or a 3.825 in science.

Clue 3: The only possibilities for science are that Salomi got a 3.35 or a 3.825 (not 3.65, 3.175, or 2.875); that a boy got a 3.175 or a 3.65 (use information later); and that Ryann got a 2.875 or a 3.35 (not 3.825, 3.65, or 3.175).

Clue 4: One girl earned a 3.4 or a 3.75 average in math (not 3.9, 3.55, or 3.2). Ryann earned a 3.2 or a 3.55 in math (not 3.9, 3.75, or 3.4). Combining Clue 4 and Clue 1, the only math scores for Victor and Ryann are 3.55 and 3.2, so nobody else has those.

Clue 5: The only possible combination is a 3.55 average in math and a 3.92 in reading. This average is for a girl, so eliminate 3.55 math and 3.92 reading for Pearce and Victor. Ryann had a 3.55 average in math (only one; this means she got a 3.92 in reading). Victor had a 3.2 in math (only one), so Pearce had a 3.4 in math [1, .2 higher].

Clue 6: The only possible combination is a 3.175 average in science for Victor and a 3.825 average in science for Yoshi. Salomi had a 3.35 science average (only one). Then Ryann had 2.875, and Pearce had 3.65 (only ones). Victor's reading average was not 3.74 (higher than Yoshi's); Yoshi's reading average was not 4.0.

Clue 7: Salomi had a 3.9 average in math. Yoshi had a 3.75 math average (only one).

Further Reasoning: Reviewing Clue 2, Yoshi had a 3.825 in science [6], so she had a 3.87 in reading. Victor's reading average was higher than Yoshi's [6], so he had a 4.0 reading average. Reviewing Clue 7, Salomi had 3.79 or 3.74 for reading. Add her 3.9 math and her 3.35 science averages to get 7.25. If you try adding 3.79 to 7.25, you will get 11.04, which divided by 3 is 3.68, which was her G.P.A., so she had a 3.79 average in reading. Pearce had a 3.74 average in reading (only one).

Answers: Pearce, 3.4 math, 3.65 science, 3.74 reading, 3.597 G.P.A.; Ryann, 3.55 math, 2.875 science, 3.92 reading, 3.448 G.P.A.; Salomi, 3.9 math, 3.35 science, 3.79 reading, 3.68 G.P.A.; Victor, 3.2 math, 3.175 science, 4.0 reading, 3.458 G.P.A.; Yoshi; 3.75 math, 3.825 science, 3.87 reading, 3.815 G.P.A. Yoshi's G.P.A. was the highest.

Don't Freeze These Cubes   p. 40

Calculations: Squared: 4, 9, 16, 25; cubed: 8, 27, 64, 125; biquadratic: 16, 81, 256, 625.

Clue 1: Karyl's single number was not 5, and Richard's single number was not 2. Karyl's cube was not 125, and Richard's cube was not 8. Karyl's square was not 4, and Richard's square was not 25.

Clue 2: Karyl's single was not 5 [1], so Donna's square was not 25, and Jeff's cube was not 125. The only possible combinations are (Karyl) 2 x (Donna) 4 = (Jeff) 8; (Karyl) 3 x (Donna) 9 = (Jeff) 27; and (Karyl) 4 x (Donna) 16 = (Jeff) 64. Use information later.

Clue 3: Jeff's single number was not 5, and Karyl's single number was not 2. Karyl's single number was not 5 [1], so it was 4 or 3; then Jeff's single number was 3 or 2 (smaller than Karyl's). Jeff's square was not 25, but Karyl's was (only one). Jeff's biquadratic number was not 625 (largest), and Karyl's biquadratic number was not 16 (smallest). From Clue 2, because Karyl's single number was not 2, Donna's square was not 4, and Jeff's cube was not 8.

Clue 4: The outcomes cannot be (Donna) 2 x (Jeff) 4 = (Richard) 8 [1] or (Donna) 5 x (Jeff) 25 [3] = (Richard) 125. So the only possibilities are (Donna) 3 x (Jeff) 9 = (Richard) 27 and (Donna) 4 x (Jeff) 16 = (Richard) 64. Eliminate 2 and 5 for Donna's single number, 4 for Jeff's square, and 125 for Richard's cube. Then Richard's single number was 5 (only one), and Richard's square was 4 (only one). Donna's cube was 125 (only one).

Clue 5: The only possibility is 16 x 16 = 256, so Jeff's biquadratic number was 16, and Richard's biquadratic number was 256.

Clue 6: The only repeated numbers were 4 and 16. Jeff did not have a single number of 4 or a square of 4, so he had a square of 16 and a biquadratic number of 16. Then Donna had 9 for her square (only one).

Clue 7: Richard's single number was 5 [4], Donna's cube was 125 [4], and 125 x 5 = 625, so Karyl's biquadratic number was 625, and Donna's biquadratic number was 81 (only one).

Further Reasoning: Reviewing Clue 2, Donna's square was 9 [6], so (Karyl's single number) 3 x (Donna's square) 9 = (Jeff's cube) 27. Then Donna's single number was 4, and Jeff's single number was 2 (only ones). Karyl's cube was 8, and Richard's cube was 64 (only ones).

Answers: Donna, 4, 9, 125, 81; Jeff, 2, 16, 27, 16; Karyl, 3, 25, 8, 625; Richard, 5, 4, 64, 256.

What Did You Call Me? p. 42

Intro: Willie and Wisewun are two different people. Make a note that the breakdown of the five rewards was that two teachers shortened subject times, one added reading time, and two gave additional time for activities. Use information later.

Clue 1: Willie [Intro, male] isn't Noitall, because Miss is a female title. Make a note that a subject was reduced by 10 min and that lunch was lengthened.

Clue 2: Mia is not Mrs. Bookish. Willie is not Mrs. Bookish. Ura is a male, and he is Mr. Wisewun. The female teachers are Bea, Ima, and Mia.

Clue 3: Bea is not Ms. Smart. Willie is not Ms. Smart, so his last name is Readit (only one).

Clue 4: Wisewun is not the one who gave 12 ½ extra min. Therefore, Ura did not give 12 ½ extra min. Make a note that 12 ½ min was an increase in a subject [Intro; must be reading].

Clue 5: Mia did not reward the class with 7 ½, 10, or 12 ½ min. Make a note that break was extended by 15 min, lunch was lengthened [1], two subjects were taught for less time [Intro], and reading was extended by 12 ½ min [Intro].

Clue 6: The male teachers are Ura Wisewun and Willie Readit. No females match up with 7 ½ min or 12 ½ min. Willie matches up with 12 ½ min (only one), so Ura matches up with 7 ½ min (only one).

Clue 7: Ima is not Mrs. Bookish; Bea is Mrs. Bookish (only one). Bea Bookish and Ima do not match up with 15 min, because that was the time given for extra break [5]. Mia matches up with 15 min (only one).

Clue 8: Less time was taken away from math, so math was shortened by 5 min, and spelling was shortened by 10 min.

Further Reasoning: Reviewing Clue 1, the longer times were given for break, lunch, and reading, and the shorter times were given for spelling and math. Mia matches up with 15 min, which matches up with a longer break [5], so she is not Miss Noitall [1, 7 ½ min extra lunch or 10 min less spelling]. Then Mia is Ms. Smart, so Ima is Miss Noitall (only one). Ima Noitall did not give 7 ½ min more for lunch [6, Ura], so she gave 10 min less for a subject [1, spelling]. Then Bea gave 5 min less for a subject (math, only one).

Answers: Bea Bookish, 5 min; Ima Noitall, 10 min; Mia Smart, 15 min; Ura Wisewun, 7 ½ min; Willie Readit, 12 ½ min.

I'm a Computer Nut p. 43

Clue 1: Amata, Bonnie, and Elena [Intro, girls] do not match up with mrrogers1928, fasttyper176, or PowerPoint. Remember that you cannot conclude yet that mrrogers1928 or fasttyper176 matches up with PowerPoint.

Clue 2: This clue refers to three different girls: the one who uses a search engine, the one whose password is butterfly132, and Amata. Amata does not match up with search engine or butterfly132. Chris, Damien, and Florian do not match up with butterfly132 or search engine [Intro, boys].

Clue 3: This clue refers to six different people. Damien and Elena do not use a search engine or the Internet, and their passwords are not yogurt396 or fasttyper176. Bonnie uses a search engine (only one). The one who uses a search engine (Bonnie) and the one who uses the Internet are not the ones with yogurt396 and fasttyper176 as their passwords. Eliminate yogurt396 for Bonnie. Use information later.

Clue 4: Chris, Damien, and Florian do not use yogurt396 as their passwords, and they do not use Inspiration [Intro, boys]. These are Amata's password (only one) and program.

Clue 5: No boy uses Excel; Elena does (only one). No boy has mtdew1948 as his password. Elena uses Excel, so she does not have mtdew1948 as her password. Bonnie does (only one), and Elena's password is butterfly132 (only one).

Clue 6: Chris does not use PowerPoint, and his password is not mrrogers1928.

Clue 7: Chris's password is not fasttyper176, and he does not use Picasa. Then Chris's password is decoder405, and he uses the Internet (only ones). Florian's password is fasttyper176, and Damien's is mrrogers1928 (only ones). Fasttyper176 (Florian) does not match up with Picasa. Florian uses PowerPoint, and Damien uses Picasa.

Answers: Amata, yogurt396, Inspiration; Bonnie, mtdew1948, search engine; Chris, decoder405, Internet; Damien, mrrogers1928, Picasa; Elena, butterfly132, Excel; Florian, fasttyper176, PowerPoint.

Got My Numbers? p. 44

Calculations: Phones: 316-4067 = 27; 526-1439 = 30; 815-1593 = 32; 472-6951 = 34; 942-6538 = 37. Houses: 1203 is divisible by 3; 1331 is divisible by 11; 3437 is divisible by 7; 4985 is divisible by 5; and 6416 is divisible by 2, 4 and 8.

Clue 1: Delynn's phone number is 526-1439 (30).

Clue 2: Carissa is not 15, 16, or 17. Emily is not 15, 16, or 17. The others are not 13 or 14.

Clue 3: Abrah and Emily have either 316-4067 or 942-6538. Nobody else has these phone numbers.

Clue 4: Delynn's digits add up to 30 [1], so she is 15 years old.

Clue 5: The 13-year-old's house is 3437 (divisible by 7). Make a note of this. It isn't Delynn [4, she is 15].

Clue 6: The 17-year-old's house is 1203. Make a note of this. It isn't Delynn [4, she is 15].

Clue 7: Abrah is house number 4985 (divisible by 5). She is not house number 1203, which is the 17-year-old's house [6], so Abrah is not 17; she's 16 (only one), and Whitney is 17 (only one). Abrah's phone number is 316-4067 (27). Emily's phone number is 942-6538 (37; only one).

Clue 8: The 14-year-old's house is 1331 (divisible by 11). Make a note of this. It isn't Delynn [4, she is 15]. Delynn is house number 6416 (only one).

Clue 9: The phone number 815-1593 (sum of 32) matches up with the house number 1331 (divisible by 11). Emily's phone number is not 815-1593 [3], so she does not live in house 1331; and house 1331 is the 14-year-old's house [8], so Emily is not 14 years old. She is 13 (only one), and Carissa is 14.

Further Reasoning: Because Emily is 13 years old, she lives at house number 3437 [5]. Because Carissa is 14 years old, she lives at house number 1331 [8]. Then she has the phone number 815-1593, which has the sum of 32 [9]. Whitney is the 17-year-old at house number 1203 [6] with the phone number 472-6951 (only ones).

Answers: Abrah, 16, 316-4067, 4985; Carissa,14, 815-1593, 1331; Delynn, 15, 526-1439, 6416; Emily, 13, 942-6538, 3437; Whitney, 17, 472-6951, 1203.

Sudoku Solutions p. 46

Clue 1: Debra's, Ramon's, and Underwood's numbers are larger in Puzzle 3 than in Puzzle 2 (less than 9), which are larger than those in Puzzle 1 (less than 8). The 8 in Puzzle 1 cannot be theirs; it is Maria's. Nobody has the same number in any puzzle [Intro], so Maria is not 8 in Puzzle 3.

Clue 2: This is four different people: Ramon, the one who gets 5 in Puzzle 2, the one who gets 6 in Puzzle 3, and the one who gets 4 in Puzzle 1, so Ramon does not match up with any of these.

Clue 3: Maria [1] and Ramon [2] do not get 4 in Puzzle 1, so they do not get 7 in Puzzle 2.

Clue 4: In Puzzle 2, Ramon (not 7 or 5) gets 3, and Maria gets 2. Nobody has the same number in any puzzle, so Ramon does not get 3 in Puzzle 1; he gets 1 (only one).

Clue 5: Debra and Underwood both have 3 and 4 as possibilities in Puzzle 1, so Debra gets 3, and Underwood gets 4. Nobody gets the same number in any puzzle, so Underwood does not get 4 in Puzzle 3. Debra and Underwood both have 5 and 7 as possibilities in Puzzle 2, so Debra gets 5, and Underwood gets 7. Underwood gets 4 in Puzzle 1 and 7 in Puzzle 2, but he does not get 9 in Puzzle 3 [3]. Maria does not get 5 in Puzzle 2 (Debra does), so she gets 6 in Puzzle 3 [2]. Underwood gets 8 in Puzzle 3 (only one).

Further Reasoning: Reviewing Clue 1, Debra's number in Puzzle 3 is larger than her number in Puzzle 2 (which is 5), so she gets 9 in Puzzle 3, and Ramon gets 4 (only one).

Answers: Debra, 3 (Puzzle 1), 5 (Puzzle 2), 9 (Puzzle 3); Maria, 8 (Puzzle 1), 2 (Puzzle 2), 6 (Puzzle 3); Ramon, 1 (Puzzle 1), 3 (Puzzle 2), 4 (Puzzle 3); Underwood, 4 (Puzzle 1), 7 (Puzzle 2), 8 (Puzzle 3).

Pen Pal Pursuits   p. 48

Calculations: Distances from the cities are 3.25 mi, 4 mi, 5.75 mi, 6.5 mi, and 8.6 mi.

Clue 1: Fiona lives in Topeka, KS. Willie has either nine or 12 cousins (three more than someone), so he does not have four, six, or eight cousins.

Clue 2: Kenton and Willie do not live in Boise or Concord; they live in Hartford and Raleigh, so Darrion and Iris do not live in Hartford or Raleigh. Kenton and Willie do not have thee or five family members. Kenton and Willie do not live 8.6 mi (45,408 ft) from a city. Darrion lives farther than them (at least two people), so he does not live the two closest distances, 3.25 mi (17,160 ft) and 4 mi (21,120 ft).

Clue 3: Willie has six family members and does not live 4 mi from the city. The one who lives 4 mi from a city has five family members.

Clue 4: Willie lives 3.25 mi (17,160 ft) from the city, and Kenton lives 6.5 mi (34,320 ft) from the city. Darrion lives 8.6 mi (45,408 ft) from the city [2, farther than Kenton]. Willie has six family members [3], so Darrion has three family members. Darrion has eight or 12 cousins; Kenton has four or six cousins.

Clue 5: Iris does not live in Concord, New Hampshire, so she lives in Boise, Idaho, and Darrion lives in Concord (only one). Kenton does not live in Raleigh, North Carolina, so he lives in Hartford, Connecticut, and Willie lives in Raleigh (only one).

Clue 6: Iris does not live 4 mi (21,120 ft) from the city; she lives 5.75 mi from it (only one), and Fiona lives 4 mi (21,120 ft) from the city. Fiona has five family members [3, 4 mi]. The only cousin difference of one is nine for Willie and eight for the other. Iris and Fiona do not have eight cousins; Darrion does (only one). Kenton has four cousins [4, Darrion has twice as many]. Fiona has 12 cousins [1, Fiona does not have three fewer than Willie, who has nine]. Iris has six cousins (only one).

Clue 7: Iris is from Idaho [5], so she has seven family members (only one that is two more than Fiona), Fiona has five, and Kenton has four (only ones)

Answers: Darrion, three family members, eight cousins, 8.6 mi, Concord; Fiona, five family members, 12 cousins, 4 mi, Topeka; Iris, seven family members, six cousins, 5.75 mi, Boise; Kenton, four family members, four cousins, 6.5 mi, Hartford; Willie, six family members, nine cousins, 3.25 mi, Raleigh.

Which Will Be My Alma Mater? p. 50

Clue 1: The possible combinations are $9,488 tuition and fees + $9,664 room and board = $19,152 for Washington State and $43,304 tuition and fees + $10,570 room and board = $53,874 for Columbia. Use information later.

Clue 2: Noriko's school charges $2,807 for books and supplies.

Clue 3: Jamaal's school does not charge $900 for personal expenses or $936 for books and supplies. Faithe's school does not charge $2,392 for personal expenses or $1,126 for books and supplies.

Clue 4: Jamaal's school is not St. Olaf, $36,800, or $43,304 for tuition and fees. Tuition and fees at St. Olaf cost either $23,096 ($13,608 higher than $9,488) or $36,800 ($13,704 higher than $23,096). Use information later.

Clue 5: Noriko's school does not charge $9,664 for room and board. Jamaal's school does not charge $9,664 for room and board.

Clue 6: One student's school charges $1,000 for books and supplies and $900 for personal expenses. Jamaal will not have to pay $900 [3], so he does not match up with $1,000. Then he will pay $1,126 for books and supplies (only one). Noriko will not have to pay $1,000 [2], so she will not pay $900 for personal expenses.

Clue 7: The possible combinations are $900 x 5 = $4,500; $1,500 x 5 = $7,500; $2,108 x 5 = $10,540; and $2,392 x 5 = $11,960. The closest is that Noriko's room and board costs $10,570 and Kipling's personal expenses cost $2,108.

Faithe's personal expenses cost $900 (only one). Then Faithe's books cost $1,000 [6]. Kipling's books cost $936 (only one).

Clue 8: Jamaal will not spend $8,500 on room and board (least), and he will not spend $9,664 [5] or $10,570 [7, Noriko], so he will spend $9,084 (only one). Faithe will spend $8,500. Kipling will spend $9,664 for room and board (only one). Both Noriko's and Jamaal's options for personal expenses are $1,500 and $2,392. Jamaal will spend more, so he will spend $2,392, and Noriko will spend $1,500. Faithe will spend $900 on personal expenses (only one).

Further Reasoning: Reviewing Clue 1, Kipling's room and board will cost $9,664 [8], so tuition and fees will cost $9,488, totaling $19,152 for Washington. Noriko's room and board will cost $10,570 [7], so tuition and fees will cost $43,304, totaling $53,874 for Columbia. Jamaal will pay $23,096 for tuition and fees (only one). He will not go to St. Olaf [4], so he will go to Colorado. Faithe's tuition and fees cost $36,800 (only one), and she will go to St. Olaf.

Answers: Faithe, St. Olaf College, $36,800 tuition and fees, $8,500 room and board, $1,000 books, $900 personal expenses; Jamaal, Colorado State University, $23,096 tuition and fees, $9,084 room and board, $1,126 books, $2,392 personal expenses; Kipling, Washington State University, $9,488 tuition and fees, $9,664 room and board, $936 books, $2,108 personal expenses; Noriko, Columbia University, $43,304 tuition and fees, $10,570 room and board, $2,807 books, $1,500 personal expenses.

What's My Total?   p. 52

Intro: Nobody's first and last names are the same, so there is no Andrew Andrew, Burke Burke, Chandler Chandler, or Wallace Wallace.

Clue 1: Burke's last name is not Wallace. Chandler's last name is not Andrew.

Clue 2: Andrew got a 15% discount (on perfume). Andrew's last name is not Wallace (this person got a 12% discount). Then Chandler's last name is Wallace (only one), so Chandler got a 12% discount.

Clue 3: Andrew's last name is not Chandler, because he bought perfume [2], not a picture frame, so his price was not $8.50. Wallace's price was $8.00, and the person whose last name is Chandler paid $8.50, so Wallace's last name is not Chandler. Then Burke's last name is Chandler, Wallace's last name is Andrew, and Andrew's last name is Burke (only ones). Then Burke Chandler paid $8.50.

Clue 4: Wallace's flowers [3] were 10% off; then Burke's frame was on an 8% discount (only one). Andrew got perfume [2], so he didn't get the candle or pay $9.50; he paid $9.00, and Chandler paid $9.50 (only ones).

Answers: Andrew Burke, $9.00, 15%, $7.65; Burke Chandler, $8.50, 8%, $7.82; Chandler Wallace, $9.50, 12%, $8.36; Wallace Andrew, $8.00, 10%, $7.20.

Our Loyal Fans

Clue 1: The Cardinals did not have a home average of 30,385; 37,499; or 37,610. The Cubs' average was not 46,491; 30,385; or 37,499. The Rangers' average was not 40,755 or 46,491. The Red Sox did not have an average of 40,755 or 46,491. The order of the Rangers and the Red Sox is not known.

Clue 2: The only totals that work are that the Yankees had 3,765,807 in attendance and the Cardinals had 3,301,218.

Clue 3: The Cubs did not have the fewest in attendance (2,505,171). The Red Sox were not highest after the Cardinals and the Yankees (3,062,973).

Clue 4: The only road averages with a difference of 237 are 32,272 (Cubs) and 32,035 (Giants).

Clue 5: The only combinations with a difference of 5,325 for Red Sox are a road average of 32,285 and a home average of 37,610.

Clue 6: The Cubs and Giants did not have 30,687 road averages [4], so they did not have 40,755 home averages. Then the Cubs had a 37,814 home average (only one). The Rangers did not have a 40,755 home average [1], so they did not have a 30,687 road average.

Clue 7: The 2010 World Series was between the Giants and the Rangers [Intro], so one of those teams had 2,505,171 and one had 3,037,443. No other teams had those numbers. The Red Sox had 3,046,445 (only one); then the Cubs had 3,062,973 (only one).

Clue 8: The Yankees' road average was higher than the Cardinals' and the Rangers' (meaning that it must be 34,939). The Rangers' road average was 26,565 (only one), and the Cardinals' was 30,687 (only one). Because the Cardinals had 30,687, they also had a 40,755 home average [6].

Clue 9: The Yankees had the highest total attendance [2], so they also had the highest home average (46,491). The Rangers had the lowest total attendance (2,505,171) and the lowest home average (30,385). The Giants had 3,037,443 total attendance (only one) and 37,499 home average (only one).

Answers: Cardinals, 3,301,218 (total); 30,687 (road); 40,755 (home). Cubs, 3,062,973 (total); 32,272 (road); 37,814 (home). Giants, 3,037,443 (total); 32,035 road; 37,499 (home). Rangers, 2,505,171 (total); 26,565 (road); 30,385 (home); Red Sox, 3,046,445 (total); 32,285 (road); 37,610 (home). Yankees, 3,765,807 (total); 34,939 (road); 46,491 (home).

Math Bafflers: Logic Puzzles That Use Real-World Math • Grades 6–8

94

Calculations: Jogging: ⅛ mi = 220 yd, ⅕ mi = 352 yd, ¼ mi = 440 yd, ⅜ mi = 660 yd, ⅗ mi = 1,056 yd. Jumping: 4 yd = 12 ft, 6 yd = 18 ft, 9 yd = 27 ft, 12 yd = 36 ft, 15 yd = 45 ft. Hopping: 3 ft = 36 in., 4 ft = 48 in., 7 ft = 84 in., 11 ft = 132 in., 15 ft = 180 in.

Clue 1: Terrence jogged ⅜ or ¼ mi; Elicia jogged ¼ or ⅛ mi.

Clue 2: The 15-ft hop matches up with the 15-yd. jump. Use information later.

Clue 3: Nolan is 5 or 6 years old, and Kyzer is 15 or 18 years old. Elicia is 5 or 6 years old, and Terrence is 15 or 18 years old. Phaedra is 10 years old (only one).

Clue 4: A girl is 6 years old (clue says *she* jumped.), so Elicia [Intro, girl], not Nolan, is 6 years old. Nolan is 5 years old (only one). Elicia hopped 11 ft and jumped 12 ft (only difference of 1 ft).

Clue 5: Because 3 ft is ⅑ of 27 ft and 4 ft is ⅑ of 36 ft, Kyzer and Phaedra hopped 36 in. (3 ft) and 48 in. (4 ft). Nolan and Terrence hopped 84 in. (7 ft) and 180 in. (15 ft). Kyzer and Phaedra jumped 27 ft and 36 ft; Nolan and Terrence jumped 18 ft and 45 ft.

Clue 6: Either Kyzer or Terrence is 15 years old, so one of them jogged ⅗ mi (1,056 yd). Terrence did not jog ⅗ mi [1]; Kyzer did, so he jumped 1,056 yd ÷ 88 = 12 yd. Kyzer's jump was 12 yd (36 ft), his hop was 4 ft (48 in.) [5, ⅑ of jump], and he is 15 years old. Phaedra's jump was 9 yd (27 ft; only one) and her hop was 3 ft (36 in.) [5, ⅑ of jump]. Terrence is 18 years old (only one).

Clue 7: Terrence is 18 years old [6], so he jogged ¼ mi (440 yd) and jumped 18 ft [6, Kyzer jumped 36 ft]. Nolan jumped 45 ft (only one); then he also jumped 180 in. (15 ft) [2, 15 ft and 15 yd]. Terrence hopped 84 in. (7 ft; only one). Elicia jogged 220 yd [1, ⅛ mi less than Terrence].

Clue 8: Phaedra is 10 years old [3], so she jogged 352 yd (⅕ mi), and Nolan jogged 660 yd (⅜ mi).

Answers: Elicia, 220-yd jog, 12-ft jump, 132-in. hop, 6 years old; Kyzer, 1,056-yd jog, 36-ft jump, 48-in. hop, 15 years old; Nolan, 660-yd jog, 45-ft jump, 180-in. hop, 5 years old; Phaedra, 352-yd jog, 27-ft jump, 36-in. hop, 10 years old; Terrence, 440-yd jog, 18-ft jump, 84-in. hop, 18 years old.

Shape Up: Double Workout (Part I) p. 58

Clue 1: One student identified the nine-sided nonagon. He measured 2.2 cm as the length of the sides of a shape, but it was not the nonagon. Use information later.

Clue 2: One student mistakenly called the seven-sided shape an octagon. He or she measured the seven-sided shape and got 1.9 cm for the side length. Use information later.

Clue 3: Eliminate the six-sided shape for Enola.

Clue 4: Either Darshan or Seth named the nine-sided nonagon correctly, so eliminate nine and nonagon for Enola, Lani, and Tierra. Either Darshan or Seth matches up with heptagon, so Enola, Lani, and Tierra do not match up with heptagon. Then Darshan and Seth did not name the pentagon, hexagon, or octagon. Either Darshan or Seth measured sides with a length of 2.2 cm [1].

Clue 5: Lani's figure had five sides. Lani did not name the hexagon or the octagon, so she named the pentagon (only one).

Clue 6: Darshan was asked about the eight-sided figure and guessed it was a heptagon (incorrect). Eliminate eight sides for Enola and Tierra. Enola named the figure with seven sides, and Tierra named the figure with six sides (only ones). Seth correctly said that the nine-sided figure was a nonagon [1, 4].

Clue 7: Eliminate 2.8 cm for Darshan.

Clue 8: Lani measured 1.5 cm for the sides of the shape she chose, not for the one she was asked about.

Clue 9: Seth matches up with nine sides and nonagon.

Further Reasoning: Reviewing Clue 1, Seth measured 2.2-cm sides. Reviewing Clue 2, Enola's assigned figure had seven sides; she said it was an octagon (incorrect) and measured its sides at 1.9 cm. Tierra's shape was a hexagon (only one). Darshan measured sides of 1.8 cm (only one), and Tierra measured sides of 2.8 cm (only one).

Answers: Darshan, eight sides, heptagon, 1.8 cm; Enola, seven sides, octagon, 1.9 cm; Lani, five sides, pentagon, 1.5 cm; Seth, nine sides, nonagon, 2.2 cm; Tierra, six sides, hexagon, 2.8 cm.

Shape Up: Double Workout (Part II)   p. 60

Intro: Only two students (Darshan and Enola) measured their assigned shapes (Darshan's had eight sides, and Enola's had seven sides, Part I). Lani, Seth, and Tierra did not measure their assigned shapes from before, so Lani's shape did not have five sides (Part I) or seven or eight sides (Enola's and Darshan's shapes). Seth's shape did not have nine sides (Part I) or seven or eight sides. Tierra's shape did not have six sides (Part I) or seven or eight sides.

Clue 1: The nonagon's perimeter measured 13.5 cm, and 13.5 ÷ 9 = 1.5-cm sides (note for later). Seth had a nonagon in Part I, but not in Part II, so he did not have a 13.5-cm perimeter or 1.5-cm sides. You can also eliminate these for Darshan and Enola (neither had a nine-sided figure).

Clue 2: Seth did not measure a 2.8-cm side or a 14.0-cm perimeter. Because 14 ÷ 2.8 = 5, Seth did not measure the five-sided pentagon. His figure had six sides (only one). Lani's had nine sides, and Tierra's had five sides (only ones).

Clue 3: Calculate 14.4 ÷ 1.8 to figure out that this figure had eight sides. Darshan was assigned the eight-sided figure in Part I and chose the eight-sided figure in Part II, so Darshan measured a 1.8-cm side and calculated a 14.4-cm perimeter.

Clue 4: Tierra measured 2.8 cm per side. She had a figure with five sides (pentagon) [2]. Because 2.8 x 5 = 14, her figure's perimeter was 14.0 cm.

Further Reasoning: Reviewing Clue 1, the nonagon (nine sides) had a 13.5-cm perimeter and 1.5-cm sides. Lani's figure had nine sides [2], so she measured a 1.5-cm side and a 13.5-cm perimeter. Enola's figure had seven sides [Part I]. She had either a 13.2-cm or a 13.3-cm perimeter and either a 1.9-cm or a 2.2-cm length. Calculate the options until you get the one that gives you seven sides: 13.2 ÷ 1.9 = 6.9; 13.2 ÷ 2.2 = 6; 13.3 ÷ 2.2 = 6.05; 13.3 ÷ 1.9 = 7 (correct). Enola measured 1.9-cm sides and a 13.3-cm perimeter. Then Seth measured 2.2 cm for side length and 13.2 cm for perimeter (only ones).

Answers: Darshan, eight sides, 1.8 cm (side length), 14.4 cm (perimeter); Enola, seven sides, 1.9 cm (side length), 13.3 cm (perimeter); Lani, nine sides, 1.5 cm (side length), 13.5 cm (perimeter); Seth, six sides, 2.2 cm (side length), 13.2 cm (perimeter); Tierra, five sides, 2.8 cm (side length), 14.0 cm (perimeter).

Miles for Moms   p. 62

Clue 1: Graham's mom drove 100 mi. Graham's mom left at 4:00, 4:30, or 5:00. Aiden's mom left at 5:00, 5:30, or 6:00. Graham's mom did not leave at 5:30 or 6:00. Aiden's mom did not leave at 4:00 or 4:30.

Clue 2: Graham's mom drove 100 mi [1], so her cargo was not milk (matches up with 300 mi) or logs (matches up with 500 mi).

Clue 3: Jackson's mom did not haul milk (the person who hauled milk left before, so she did not drive 300 mi, either). Jackson's mom left at 5:00, 5:30, or 6:00. The one who hauled milk left at 4:00, 4:30, or 5:00. Jackson's mom did not leave at 4:00 or 4:30.

Clue 4: The 200-mi driver left at 4:00, 4:30, or 5:00; the milk driver left at 4:30, 5:00, or 5:30; and Graham's mom left at 5:00, 5:30, or 6:00. But Graham's mom did not leave at 5:30 or 6:00 [1], so she left at 5:00, the milk driver left at 4:30, and the 200-mi driver left at 4:00. Aiden's mom left 60 min after Graham's mom [1], so Aiden's mom left at 6:00. Jackson's mom left at 5:30

(only one). Aiden's mom left at 6:00, so she did not haul milk (4:30) or drive 200 mi (4:00), and Jackson's mom (5:30) did not drive 200 mi.

Clue 5: The person who hauled milk left at 4:30 [4], so bread matches up with 5:00. Graham's mom left at 5:00 [4], so she hauled bread.

Clue 6: Carter's mom did not drive 200 mi or 500 mi (so she did not haul logs), and she did not haul mail or gasoline. She hauled milk (only one), so she drove 300 mi and left at 4:30. Elijah's mom left at 4:00 and drove 200 mi (only ones). She did not drive 500 mi, so she did not haul logs.

Clue 7: Aiden's mom left at 6:00 [4], so the 500-mi driver left at 5:30 [4, Jackson's mom]; so Jackson's mom hauled logs and drove 500 miles. Aiden's mom drove 400 mi (only one).

Clue 8: The 4:00 driver was Elijah's mom [6], so Elijah's mom did not haul gasoline; she hauled mail (only one), and Aiden's mom hauled gasoline (only one).

Answers: Aiden's mom, 400 mi, gasoline, 6:00; Carter's mom, 300 mi, milk, 4:30; Elijah's mom, 200 mi, mail, 4:00; Graham's mom, 100 mi, bread, 5:00; Jackson's mom, 500 mi, logs, 5:30.

Climb Ev'ry Mountain   p. 64

Clue 1: Harney Peak is in SD. Harney Peak is not 1,979 ft or 4,139 ft (less than 5,280 ft), so SD does not match up with 1,979 ft or 4,139 ft. Bigstone Lake is 966 ft. Use information later.

Clue 2: The Kootenai River is .34 mi (1,800 ft). Eliminate the Kootenai River and 1,800 ft for KY and MI.

Clue 3: Death Valley is −282 ft. Use information later.

Clue 4: Black Mountain is in KY, and ¾ mile works out to 3,960 ft, so Black Mountain is a little more than 3,960 ft (4,139 ft). SD's lowest point is 966 ft, which is Bigstone Lake [1].

Clue 5: This clue refers to five states, so none of these pieces of information match up together. CA is not where the Kootenai River is, and it does not match up with 257 ft, Harney Peak [1, SD], or 1,979 ft. Then the Kootenai River is in MT (only one), so MT matches up with 1,800 ft [2], but it does not match up with 257 ft, Harney Peak, or 1,979 ft. Then MI matches up with 1,979 ft (only one), so MI does not match up with 257 ft. Then 257 ft matches up with KY (only one).

Clue 6: Granite Peak is in MT and does not match up with 1,979 ft (MI), 4,139 ft (KY), or 7,242 ft (2 mi = 10,560 ft).

Clue 7: Mount Whitney is in CA. Mount Arvon is in MI (only one). Mount Whitney is 14,494 ft, so CA matches up with 14,494 ft. Then MT matches up with 12,799 ft, and SD matches up with 7,242 ft (only ones).

Clue 8: Eliminate the Mississippi River for MI.

Further Reasoning: Reviewing Clue 3, Death Valley is the lowest elevation, so it is −282 ft below sea level. Death Valley is 84.6 mi from Mount Whitney and is in the same state, which is CA [7], so Death Valley is in CA. Then the 572-ft elevation is in MI, the Mississippi River is in KY, and Lake Erie is in MI (only ones).

Answers: CA, Death Valley, −282 ft, Mount Whitney, 14,494 ft; KY, Mississippi River, 257 ft, Black Mountain, 4,139 ft; MI, Lake Erie, 572 ft, Mount Arvon, 1,979 ft; MT, Kootenai River, 1,800 ft, Granite Peak, 12,799 ft; SD, Bigstone Lake, 966 ft, Harney Peak, 7,242 ft.

What's Your Number? p. 66

Calculations: Ages add up to 4, 5, 3, 6, and 8; birthdays add up to 12, 24, 9, 20, and 36; and bank accounts add up to 40, 32, 18, 30, and 42.

Clue 1: Mason does not match up with February 10 (6), March 21 (24), October 26 (36), 5639-7253 (40), or 3509-8241 (32). Mason is a male (clue says *his*).

Clue 2: Thad does not match up with 6201-2016 (18), 2036-5743 (30), 5480-4975 (42), May 4 (9), or August 12 (20).

Clue 3: Age number possibilities are 6 (60) and 8 (62) for Kirk and 3 (30) and 4 (22) for Ellie. This would mean that Ellie's birthday number is 9 or 16 (the squares of 3 and 4), but there is no 16, so her birthday number must be 9 (May 4), which means that her birthday number is 3 (30). Kirk's age number is 6 (age 60). Mason's birthday is August 12 (only one).

Clue 4: Thad is a male (clues say *his*). Ellie is the daughter [3], and Kirk is the father [3], so Cindy is the mother, and her age is 62 (age number 8). Thad is 22 years old. Mason is 23 years old (only one).

Clue 5: The father's (Kirk's) birthday number is 12, 24, or 36, so it must be 12 (February 10), and Thad's birthday number must be either 24 or 36 (multiple of 12).

Clue 6: Cindy's age number is 8, so Thad's bank account number is either 40 or 32.

Clue 7: Ellie's birthday number is 9, and Mason's is 20, so Cindy's and Kirk's bank account numbers cannot be 18 (6201-2016) or 40 (5639-7253; multiples of 9 and 20).

Clue 8: Cindy's age number is 8, so her birthday number is not 36. It is 24 (March 21). Her bank account number is not 42 or 30; it is 32 (only one). Thad's birthday is October 26, and Thad's bank account number is 40 (5639-7253; only ones). Ellie's age number is 3, so her birthday number is 9 (May 4), and her bank account number is 18, 30, or 42. Kirk's age number is 6, and Kirk's bank number is 18, 30, or 42. Mason's age number is 5, so his bank account number is 30 (2036-5743). Then Kirk's bank account number is 42 (5480-4975), and Ellie's bank account number is 18 (6201-2016; only ones).

Answers: Cindy, 62, March 21, 3509-8241; Ellie, 30, May 4, 6201-2016; Kirk, 60, February 10, 5480-4975; Mason, 23, August 12, 2036-5743; Thad, 22, October 26, 5639-7253.

Take 5: Game 1   p. 68

Intro: Lionel scored 20, which is 6 + 5 + 4 + 3 + 2. Eliminate 1 in each turn for Lionel.

Clue 1: Janette did not score 20 [Intro, Lionel] or 15. Maya did not score 20 or 19 [Intro].

Clue 2: Lionel rolled a 4 during some turn (one or three), but not during turns two, four, or five.

Clue 3: Tabitha rolled a 6 in turn two. Then she did not roll a 6 in turns one, three, four, or five [Intro].

Clue 4: Greer rolled a 5 during some turn (two or three), but not during turns one, four, or five.

Clue 5: Possibilities for Lionel are 6, 5, or 4 in turn one; 5, 4, or 3 in turn five; and 4, 3, or 2 in turn four [Intro, no 1s]; so eliminate 2 and 3 in turn one, 2 and 6 in turn five, and 5 and 6 in turn four. He did not roll a 4 in turn four [2], so he did not roll a 5 in turn five or a 6 in turn one. He did not roll a 4 in turn five [2], so he did not roll a 5 in turn one or a 3 in turn four. He rolled a 4 in turn one, a 2 in turn four, and a 3 in turn five (only ones), so he did not roll a 2, a 3 or a 4 in turns two or three. Then he rolled a 5 in turn two (only one), so he did not roll a 5 in turn three. He rolled a 6 in turn 3 (only ones).

Clue 6: Eliminate all 5s for Janette. Then she rolled 1 + 2 + 3 + 4 + 6 = 16. Eliminate all 2s for Greer. Then he rolled 1 + 3 + 4 + 5 + 6 = 19. Greer rolled a 5 in turn three [4, he rolled a 5 during a turn that was not one, four, or five, and Lionel rolled a 5 in turn two].

Clue 7: Cole rolled a 1 in turn one, a 2 in turn two, and a 3 in turn three, and Cole did not roll a 1, a 2, or a 3 in turns four or five [Intro].

Clue 8: Greer rolled 4 + 5 + 6 = 15 in turns three, four, and five. He rolled a 5 in turn three, so he rolled a 4 or a 6 in turn four and a 4 or a 6 in turn five. He did not roll a 4 or a 6 in turns one or two. He rolled a 3 in turn one (only one), not a 3 in turn two [Intro, no same number], so he rolled a 1 in turn two (only one). Greer scored 19 for the game [6].

Clue 9: Maya rolled a 2 in turn one, Janette rolled a 6 in turn one, and Tabitha rolled a 5 in turn one (only ones). Then Janette did not roll a 6 in any other turns, Maya did not roll a 2 in any other turns, and Tabitha did not roll a 5 in any other turns. Tabitha rolled a 2 during turn five. She did not roll a 2 in any other turns.

Clue 10: Maya got a total of 15 points [1, less than Janette (16)]. Cole must have a total of 17 points, and Tabitha must have a total of 18 points. To make 17, Cole rolled 1 + 2 + 3 + 5 + 6, so he did not roll a 4 in turns five or six. To make 18, Tabitha rolled 1 + 2 + 4 + 5 + 6, so she did not roll a 3 in turn four.

Clue 11: Turn four possibilities are that Maya rolled a 4, Janette rolled a 5, and Cole rolled a 6 (this does not work, because Janette did not roll 5s [6]), or that Maya rolled a 3, Janette rolled a 4, and Cole rolled a 5, which works. This means that Cole did not roll a 5 in other turns, so he rolled a 6 in turn five. Janette did not roll a 4 in other turns, so she rolled a 3 in turn two. Maya did not roll a 3 in any other turns, so she rolled a 4 in turn two. For turn four, Tabitha rolled a 1 and Greer rolled a 6 (only ones). Tabitha did not roll a 1 for any other turns, so she rolled a 4 in turn three. Greer did not roll a 6 for any other turns, so he rolled a 4 in turn five.

Further Reasoning: Janette rolled a 1 in turn five (only one). Janette did not roll a 1 in any other turns, so she rolled a 2 in turn three. Maya rolled a 1 in turn three (only one), and she did not roll a 1 in any other turns, so she rolled a 5 in turn five.

Answers: Cole, 1, 2, 3, 5, 6, total 17 points; Greer, 3, 1, 5, 6, 4, total 19 points; Janette, 6, 3, 2, 4, 1, total 16 points; Lionel, 4, 5, 6, 2, 3, total 20 points; Maya, 2, 4, 1, 3, 5, total 15 points; Tabitha, 5, 6, 4, 1, 2, total 18 points.

Take 5: Game 2   p. 70

Clue 1: Use Game 1 to mark turns 1–5 for each player. Cole did not roll 1, 2, 3, 5, or 6; Greer did not roll 3, 1, 5, 6, or 4; Janette did not roll 6, 3, 2, 4, or 1; Lionel did not roll 4, 5, 6, 2, or 3; Maya did not roll 2, 4, 1, 3, or 5; and Tabitha did not roll 5, 6, 4, 1, or 2.

Clue 2: Cole did not roll any 4s, so he rolled 1, 2, 3, 5, and 6, totaling 17. Maya did not roll any 1s, so she rolled 2, 3, 4, 5, and 6, totaling 20 points (so she won).

Clue 3: Tabitha rolled a 1, a 2, and a 3 (in some order), totaling 6, in turns one, two, and three. She did not roll 4, 5, or 6 in turns one, two, or three, and she did not roll 1, 2, or 3 in turns four or five.

Clue 4: Greer rolled a 5 in turn four, so he did not roll 5s in any other turns [Intro]. Cole rolled a 5 in turn five, so he did not roll a 5 in any other turns. In turns four and five, Tabitha rolled a 4 or a 6 (no 5s, Cole and Greer), for a total score of 1 + 2 + 3 + 4 + 6 = 16 points.

Clue 5: In Game 2, Cole scored 17, Greer did not score 19, Janette did not score 16, and Lionel did not score 20. Maya scored 20, and Tabitha scored 16.

Clue 6: Janette rolled 1, 4, 5 (not 2, 3, 6) in turns one, two, and three (in some order). She did not roll 1, 4, or 5 in turns four or five. Lionel rolled 1, 4, 5 (not 2, 3, 6) in turn one, turn two, and turn three (in some order). He did not roll 1, 4, or 5 in turn four or turn five. Cole rolled a 1 in turn four (only one), which means that he did not roll a 1 in any other turns. Greer rolled a 1 in turn five (only one), meaning that he did not roll a 1 in other turns.

Clue 7: Cole rolled a 3 in turn three (Game 1), so he rolled a 2 in Game 2. This means he did not roll a 2 in any other turns. Greer rolled a 5 in turn three of Game 1, so he rolled a 6 in Game 2; this means he did not roll a 6 for any other turns.

Clue 8: Lionel rolled a 4 in turn one (Game 1), so he rolled a 5 in turn one of Game 2; this means that he did not roll any other 5s. Lionel rolled a 3 in turn five (Game 1), so he rolled a 6 in turn five of Game 2 This means he rolled no other 6s. Then he rolled a 3 in turn four (only one). Tabitha rolled a 4 in turn five (only one). This means she rolled no other 4s, so she rolled a 6 in turn four (only one). Janette rolled a 2 in turn four (only one; no other 2s), and Maya rolled a 4 in turn four (only one; no other 4s). In turn five, Janette rolled a 3 (only one; no other 3s), and Maya rolled a 2 (only one; no other 2s).

Clue 9: Janette rolled a 3 in turn five, so she rolled a 1 in turn one (no other 1s). Greer rolled a 4 in turn one (only one; no other 4s). Tabitha rolled a 2 in turn one (only one; no other 2s). Greer rolled a 2 in turn two (only one). Greer had $4 + 2 + 6 + 5 + 1 = 18$.

Clue 10: Tabitha rolled a 1 in turn two and a 3 in turn three. Lionel rolled a 4 (only one; no other 4s) in turn two; then Janette rolled a 5 (no other 5) in turn two (only ones). Lionel rolled a 1 in turn three, and Maya rolled a 5 in turn three (only one; no other 5s). Then Janette rolled a 4 in turn three (only one; no other 4s). Janet rolled a 1 in turn one and a 5 in turn two, and Lionel rolled a 1 in turn three (only ones). Lionel had 19 points, and Janette had 15.

Clue 11: Cole rolled a 2 in turn three and a 1 in turn four, totaling 3, so he rolled a 3 in turn one (no other 3s), and a 6 in turn two (only one). Maya rolled a 6 in turn one and a 3 in turn two (only ones).

Answers: Cole, 3, 6, 2, 1, 5, total 17; Greer, 4, 2, 6, 5, 1, total 18; Janette, 1, 5, 4, 2, 3, total 15; Lionel, 5, 4, 1, 3, 6, total 19; Maya, 6, 3, 5, 4, 2, total 20; Tabitha, 2, 1, 3, 6, 4, total 16.

About the Author

Marilynn L. Rapp Buxton currently teaches talented and gifted students in grades 4–6 at Waverly-Shell Rock Community Schools in Waverly and Shell Rock, IA. She also teaches fifth and sixth graders Challenge Math, along with a self-designed curriculum of creative and critical thinking skills. She is also editor of two elementary yearbooks, and she coaches Future Problem Solving teams. She received her bachelor's degree from Iowa State University and has taken numerous graduate courses through Drake University, the University of Iowa, and the University of Northern Iowa toward her educational certifications and her K–12 gifted endorsement.

Her curriculum ideas and student projects have been featured in the *Iowa Talented and Gifted Magazine*. She authored *Math Logic Mysteries* and *More Math Logic Mysteries*, published by Prufrock Press, and is currently writing several other activity books. She is also the author of *Itsy Bitsies*, four leaflets of counted cross-stitch designs, and she was featured in *Cross Stitcher Magazine*.

She has presented at the Iowa, Wisconsin, and Minnesota Talented and Gifted Conferences; the Midwest Regional Middle Level Conference; area gifted and talented forums; and local staff in-services, and she received the Iowa Talented and Gifted Conference's Distinguished Service Award in 2008. She enjoys spending time with family, swimming, singing in a barbershop chorus and quartet, and doing Sudoku and matrix logic puzzles.

Common Core State Standards Alignment

Grade Level	Common Core State Standards in Math
Grade 5	5.OA.A Write and interpret numerical expressions.
	5.NBT.B Perform operations with multi-digit whole numbers and with decimals to hundredths.
	5.NF.B Apply and extend previous understandings of multiplication and division.
	5.MD.A Convert like measurement units within a given measurement system.
Grade 6	6.NS.B Compute fluently with multi-digit numbers and find common factors and multiples.
	6.NS.C Apply and extend previous understandings of numbers to the system of rational numbers.
	6.EE.A Apply and extend previous understandings of arithmetic to algebraic expressions.
	6.EE.B Reason about and solve one-variable equations and inequalities.
Grade 7	7.NS.A Apply and extend previous understandings of operations with fractions.
	7.EE.B Solve real-life and mathematical problems using numerical and algebraic expressions and equations.
Grade 8	8.NS.A Know that there are numbers that are not rational, and approximate them by rational numbers.
	8.EE.A Work with radicals and integer exponents.

Key: OA = Operations & Algebraic Thinking; NBT = Number & Operations in Base Ten; NF = Number & Operations--Fractions; MD = Measurement & Data; NS = The Number System; EE = Expressions & Equations

Printed in the United States
by Baker & Taylor Publisher Services